Coffee with
Uncle Reggie

与曾叔叔闲聊

我们的新生儿科教授

曾振锚著 Reginald Tsang

与曾叔叔闲聊——我们的新生儿科教授

作者 / 曾振锚
中文编辑 / 古志薇
设计排版 / Busybees Design Consultants Ltd.

版次 / 二零一八年三月初版
©2018 曾振锚

国际书号：978-1-5456-2698-6

Coffee with Uncle Reggie

by Reginald Tsang
Chinese Editor/ May Ku
Design/ Busybees Design Consultants Ltd.

ISBN 978-1-5456-2698-6

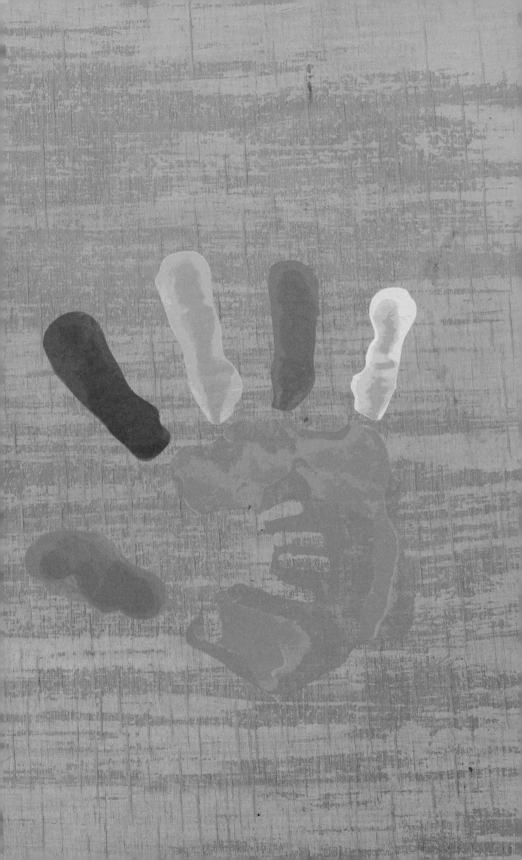

Coffee with
Uncle Reggie

与曾叔叔闲聊
我们的新生儿科教授

目录
Table of Contents

序言 6
Foreword

引言 16
Introduction

致谢 20
Acknowledgments

1. 1989 年的第一次医疗援助服务 22
A First Medical Missions Journey 1989

2. 耶和华以勒 28
Jehovah Jireh

3. 合时的癌症 34
A Good Cancer

4. 从疖子妹到女主人——
   一个童养媳的故事 40
A Child Bride: From Boils to Matriarch

5. 山中的至宝 44
Godly Heritage in a Mountain Village

6. 留下印象 50
Making an Impression

7. 烧毁家园 54
Burning Down the House

8. 导师与受教的心 60
The Guru and Teachability

9. 直起腰来的故事 68
A Kyphosis Story

10. 露西·戴安娜——
    儿童版的党书记 74
Lucy Diana, the Childhood Party Secretary

11. 油炸蜜蜂的乐趣与抽烟 82
The Joys of Deep Fried Bees Versus Smoking

12. 仿冒品 90
Counterfeits

13. 蟑螂与谦卑 94
Cockroaches and Humility

14. 新生儿 98
A Baby is Born

15. 与死亡面对面 104
A Near Death Experience

16. 基因显永恒 108
Eternity in Our Genes

17. 对亚洲人的偏见 112
Asian Stereotype

18. 亚洲人的热情好客 116
Asian Hospitality

19 辛辛那提在哪？ 122
Where is Cincinnati?

后记 128
Postscript

Foreword

It has been said that if you walk with the wise in your life, it is your honor, and you should be grateful to have met such a person in your life.

I had a "chance encounter" with Dr. Reggie Tsang in August 1994 at West China University: he was just such a wise person, who had great love and benevolence.

From that time onwards, we were partners striding together, unceasingly, in the pediatric world, and striving to set up the bridge for communication and interchange of China-American pediatric scholars. With great love and patience, Dr. Tsang personally dedicated his strengths and knowledge to the areas that needed him.

I always remember his gentle smile, but I do not remember any expression of anxiety. In any tense or anxious moments, he would smile away the problem. I remember his Mandarin was like those of Chinese ethnic origin who grew up in America, but his Putonghua was kind and gentle. He tried very hard to communicate clearly, always in a friendly tone.

I remember his physical hardship when he often traveled among many cities of China from Cincinnati, USA. It seems that at any time, he did not stop thinking and planning how to bring the best of American academics to China. And how to create the conditions for young physicians and nurses to have opportunities to learn in the USA. I know that he tried also to help meet their needs and make their stay in Cincinnati a very pleasant one, so that they could focus their energies on study, instead of being too homesick.

序言

有人曾说，如果你的人生与智慧之人相伴前行，是你的荣幸，是值得感恩的生命中的相遇。

曾振锚医生是我在 1994 年 8 月在华西大学"偶遇"的智慧之人。他不仅有智慧，而且拥有大爱大德。

自此，我们结伴前行，在儿科医学领域中不断追求，架起中美儿科学者交流的桥梁。他更以博大的爱心和恒心，身体力行地在需要他的地方奉献自己的力量和知识。

我总记得他的微笑，但记不起他曾有任何焦虑的表情。即使焦虑或者生气，他也用微笑化解。记得他说普通话的时候，是带着在美国长大的华人的语调。但他说的普通话，亲切而温柔。因为他总是尽量表达得清晰，语气和善。

记得他频频往返于中国各个城市和美国辛辛那提市的艰辛。任何时候，他似乎从来没有停止思考：如何把美国最好的学术研究带到中国；如何创造条件让年轻的中国医生和护士获得赴美国学习的机会；如何让在美国的中国医生和护士安心，让思乡之情变成学习动力。他总是提供最需要的帮助。

记得那只他总是装在挎包里的枕头。坐着时，他的腰要靠这只枕头一直垫着才不会痛……再想着长达超过十万八千里的旅途，他是怎样坐着完成飞行旅程的？在他的努力下，中国多间医院和医学院校与辛辛那提儿童医学中心开展了合作的项

I remember he was always uniquely carrying a bag that had his pillow inside, so that he could protect and support his back to prevent pain.... Just remember his very long travel distances of more than 100-thousand mile journeys, how did he manage to complete all those air travels? Through all his strenuous efforts, he established many partnership ventures between hospitals and medical schools in China and Cincinnati Children's Hospital Medical Center. He was the emissary for development of cooperative agreements between China and American pediatrics.

No, indeed he was an angel.

I remember that in 2004, his wife had a serious illness, yet while he was looking after his wife, he was always thinking about us also. In America, he edited the classic "Bible" for preterm infant clinical care, *Nutrition of the Preterm Infant: Scientific Basis and Practical Guidelines*. When he realized that this kind of specialized book was not available in China, he immediately agreed that I could translate the book into Chinese, so that we could publish the book in 2009. Under his efforts he waived any charges and copyright issues, so that Chinese pediatricians could be benefited.

I have met his wife and daughter, and they are both beautiful and kind from their deepest nature. Without saying a word, they touch your spirit. Truly, I'm very honored to have met and known Dr. Reggie, and I am very grateful.

In all the stories that Dr. Reggie has written for you in this book, it's good that you read them. They are also genuine and true. I believe that, just like me, you would be full of gratitude.

Meng MAO, MD, Professor of Pediatrics;
President, West China Second University Hospital, Sichuan University 2001-2010;
President, Chengdu Women's and Children's Central Hospital 2011-2014;
Group Leader of Child Health Care, China Pediatrics Society of
China Medical Association 2009-present

目。他是中美儿科医学合作协同发展的使者。

不，他就是天使。

记得 2004 年，他的夫人身患重病。在照顾夫人的日子里，他也始终想着我们。他在美国主编的《早产儿营养——基础与实践指南》是一本早产儿临床护理的经典。当他听说中国没有这样的专业书的时候，就立即同意我将它翻译成中文，于 2009年在中国出版。在他的努力下，免去了此书的版税，让更多的中国儿科医生受益。

我见过他的夫人，也见过他的女儿。她们从内而外洋溢出来的美丽与善良，不需言语，便可以打动你的心灵。真的，能与曾振锚医生相遇、相识，我很庆幸，也深怀感激。

曾振锚医生这本书记录的这些故事，你读，就对了——一切都是那么自然而真切。相信你一定会与我一样，充满感恩。

毛萌医生，儿科学教授
四川大学华西第二医院院长（2001-2010）
成都市妇女儿童中心医院院长（2011-2014）
中华医学会儿科学分会儿童保健学组组长（2009- 现在）

Reggie was my senior by eleven years at the Medical School, the University of Hong Kong. By the time when I was still half way through my Pediatric residency at Queen Mary Hospital where Reggie also received his early Pediatric training, he was already an internationally renowned neonatologist and guru in neonatal nutritional research. Nicknamed "Mr. Calcium" in the Pediatric world for his supremacy in calcium and vitamin D research, he was also well known to us as one of the most distinguished alumni of the University, and a role model for Pediatric trainees to follow. It was not surprising that when Reggie took early retirement from clinical practice in 1994 to devote his time to the works of MSI, the news created a shockwave of disappointment and disbelief through the Pediatric community in Hong Kong. As things turned out, Reggie's selfless and bold decision actually brought him closer to us. In the course of his many service trips to China, he often had to stop over Hong Kong, and would look us up when he did. During these short visits he always preferred staying in the small local MSI office rather than checking into a hotel. "Just to save a few dimes for the organization", so he said. Personal comfort never seemed to be his concern or else he would not have made so many difficult journeys to the rural and poverty-stricken South-western China. In those days, merely travelling to those places was physically very demanding, not to mention the hardship he had to endure living in accommodations that often lacked even the most basic daily amenities.

Having travelled numerous miles in rural China and brought education to tens of thousands of poor village children, Reggie has now "retired" again but only to take up a new project of sharing his life experience with the rest of the world. The first volume of his story book *Coffee with Uncle Reggie* is a great collection of real stories he gathered

振锚是比我早 11 年毕业的香港大学医学院师兄。当我还在玛丽医院当实习儿科医生期间，早年同样在玛丽医院接受儿科培训的振锚，已经是国际知名的新生儿专家和新生儿营养研究的权威。振锚对钙和维生素 D 有杰出的研究，令他在儿科界中有"钙先生"的昵称。他是香港大学最杰出的校友之一，也是儿科医生学习的榜样。难怪振锚在 1994 年提前退休、投入国际医疗服务机构的工作时，香港的儿科界对这消息既感震撼，又觉得难以置信。事实证明，振锚无私而大胆的决定实际上使他和我们更接近。他频繁地前往中国提供医疗服务，经常都要停留香港，这时就会来找我们。暂短停留香港时，他总是喜欢住在 MSI 的小办公室，而不是入住酒店。他说："要为组织省一点经费。"个人舒适与否，他从来不担心，否则他不会千辛万苦地前往农村和贫困的中国西南地区。当年要到这些地方，单是长途跋涉的艰苦旅途对体能的要求已非常苛刻，更别提要在缺乏最基本日常设施的地方住宿所吃的苦头。

振锚的足迹踏遍不少中国农村，并向数万名贫穷的农村小孩子带来教育的机会。他现在再次"退休"了，却以一个新的方式与世界各地的人分享他的人生经验。他第一册的 *Coffee with Uncle Reggie*，收集了他多次在亚洲和中国旅程中的真实故事。这些冒险故事充满了智慧之言和启示人生的教训，不论长者或年青人都会觉得鼓舞人心。我非常高兴振锚这次以中英文双语讲述自己的故事。以英文写作、附中文翻译的《与曾叔

from his many travels in Asia and China. They are stories of adventure, with a wealth of words of wisdom and spiritual lessons that are inspirational to all, young and old. I am most delighted that Reggie would tell more of his stories this time in a bilingual book. Written in English with Chinese translation, *Coffee with Uncle Reggie Volume 2* would be able to reach people even in rural China, people who Reggie cares so much about.

Tai-fai Fok, Pro-Vice Chancellor and Vice President,
Choh-Ming Lee Professor of Paediatrics, The Chinese University of Hong Kong

S erving others is at the heart of everything Christian. If you think serving others for a higher calling is drudgery and something to avoid, please think again. Through Dr. Reggie Tsang's many engaging vignettes you will find the Lord working through a man's life to fill it with many global friends and meaningful kingdom work. There is adventure: like eating fried bees and hanging onto a patient who fell over the fifth floor railing of a hospital. As a neonatologist, Dr. Reggie cared for the physical lives of pre-born infants, but he was also an effective "doctor of the hearts and souls" of untold children and youth, and adults, around the world. Read and be inspired to invest your life in the Lord's work just as Uncle Reggie did.

Bruce Chester, Chairman of the Board, Medical Services International, USA;
dedicated to medical missions in China

叔闲聊》，更能够接触到中国农村的读者，也就是振锚非常关心的人。

霍泰辉教授
香港中文大学副校长
卓敏儿科讲座教授

服务他人是基督徒生活的核心。如果你觉得为回应一个更高的呼召而服务他人是一件苦差和要避免的事情，请再想一想。通过曾振锚医生的许多动人小故事，你会发现主如何使用一个人的生命，让他结交世界各地的朋友，并做有意义的工作。当中有冒险的时候：例如吃油炸的蜜蜂，拉住一个要跨过医院五楼栏杆跳下去的病人。作为一名新生儿科医生，曾医生关心胎儿的身体健康，但他也是世界各地无数儿童、青少年以及成年人的"心灵医生"。请阅读曾医生的故事，并受启发，就像曾叔叔一样，将自己的生命投入主的工作中。

布鲁斯·切斯特
国际医疗服务机构美国委员会主席
致力从事中国的医疗服务工作

Coffee with Uncle Reggie contains a charming collection of stories, words skillfully woven together, not just to tell a tale, but more importantly to reflect special lessons that Uncle Reggie has learned along the way. While on this journey, he has been able to interpret his circumstances and communicate them in a way that demonstrates the goodness and greatness of the Creator and the intricacies of His creation. These tales will bring a smile to your face!

David Leung, MD;
President, MSI Professional Services, Hong Kong;
Physician, Evergreen China, Shanxi.

Uncle Reggie's stories provide vivid accounts of obstacles presented to him. Though these obstacles created many setbacks, it is always encouraging to see how Uncle Reggie has persevered. His stories have provided and inspired me, as a Christian, to always have faith in our Lord! *Coffee with Uncle Reggie* is a must-read since it is enjoyable and encouraging for all!

Elton Tong, student of Walnut Hills High School (Cincinnati);
Cincinnati Chinese Church Thai Youth Missions Team veteran

《与曾叔叔闲聊》是一连串引人入胜的故事，以文字巧妙地编织在一起，不仅仅是讲故事，更重要的是反映出曾叔叔在过程中学习到的特别教训。在这些经历中，他在理解面对的情况和演绎故事的时候，更能够把创造者的善良和伟大，以及创造的复杂精密表现出来。这些故事会使你会心微笑！

梁启予医生
香港国际医疗服务机构的专业服务总裁
中国山西永青服务中心医生

　　曾叔叔的故事生动地描述了他面对的困难。虽然这些困难带来许多挫折，但是看曾叔叔如何坚持不懈，总是令人鼓舞。作为一个基督徒，他的故事激励我永远相信我们的主！《与曾叔叔闲聊》是一本必读的书，阅读它是赏心乐事，它又能鼓励所有读者！

唐耀升
辛辛那提核桃山高中学生
辛城教会泰国青年布道队资深队员

翻译：Eileen

Introduction

Welcome to *Coffee with Uncle Reggie*, otherwise known as Uncle Reggie's Stories or Reggie Tales! *Coffee with Uncle Reggie* is written for those who are young at heart. I am 76 years old as of this writing, but have worked for decades with children and youth in America, China and Southeast Asia. Please read and enjoy the stories from my travels through 150 cities of the world! They not only reflect my life's journey, but also eternal values and my love of life and children.

For most of my life I have loved to tell stories over coffee or lunch to young people and international students, so please read this book as a conversation, while imagining that I am telling you my stories face-to-face with you.

I remember vividly a conversation in very multicultural Malaysia. One person started a story in English, and the entire roundtable of people continued the conversation in English. Then someone started saying something in Mandarin, and the entire table switched immediately into lively Mandarin. Then the conversation switched to Hakka; then Chaozhou, and then finally the story finished in Cantonese. Life is sort of like that. As you encounter different people, their stories come crashing in from all different angles, sometimes in different languages and accents, and all woven in a wonderful matrix of colors and forms.

As I weave my stories in a rather unconventional way, rather like a scrapbook, with surprises that might pop up unexpectedly, please jump in with me to my medical mission, then my ancestral roots, then the

引言

欢迎你阅读《与曾叔叔闲聊》！本书是专为那些心灵年轻的人写的。写这些文章时，我已经 76 岁了，但曾经在美国、中国和东南亚参与儿童和青少年事工几十年。请阅读并享受我旅遊过世界 150 个城市的故事！它们不仅展现了我人生的旅程，也反映出我的永恒价值观、对生活和孩子的热爱。

我大半生都喜欢在喝咖啡或午餐时向年轻人和留学生讲故事。因此，当你读这本书时，就当作在听一个对话，想像我是**面对面**给你讲故事。

我清楚记得在多文化的马来西亚有这么一场对话。一个人开始用英语讲故事，然后整个餐桌的人继续用英语交谈。有人开始用普通话说话，大家立刻转而以活泼的普通话交谈。然后谈话又换到客家话，接着是潮州话，故事最终以广东话结束。生活就是这样，当你遇到不同的人，他们的故事以各种不同的角度，有时是不同的语言和方言，编织交错成一幅美好、五彩缤纷的图像。

当我以一种非常规的方式编织我的故事，使它像一本令你有意外惊喜的剪贴簿时，请跟我一起看看我的医疗服务使命、我祖宗的故事，还有我所遇到的有趣的文化和朋友，最后回到本垒，然后……下一步又怎样？

interesting culture and friends I met, and finally back to home base, and then...what's next?

May the good Lord use this book in His wonderful ways.

Uncle Reggie
Youth For All Nations, YFAN
Seattle, USA
September 2017

愿主以祂美妙的方式使用这本书。

曾叔叔
万国青年
美国西雅图
2017 年 9 月

翻译：Eileen

Acknowledgements

I am immensely grateful to my Creator for the wonderful gifts He has given me; for my long-suffering wife Esther, and children Trevor (Elaine) and Olivia; for my mentors: especially Bruce Chester, Paul and Margaret Brand, "Richard", Mark Beadle, and Ben Walker; for many Children's Hospital research fellows from all over the world; and especially for my dear YFAN co-workers, Steve Norman, Wendy Wong, Mark Jiang, Chad McIntosh and Karen Stuckey, all of whom have given me much encouragement and joy from seeing what they are doing for the Lord. Many thanks especially to Jenny Liao for starting the first Reggie Tales website with such enthusiasm, and Felicity Tao for rejuvenating it and giving great ideas; and my faithful staff Susan Han and Robert Louie for all their many hours of hard work. The CVSG team, Peter Yang, Amy Zhao, Mary Fan, John Bascom and Mary Anne Lucas; the Translators Team, identified with each article; Hongyan Zhu for last minute translation; and the Media Team of Yang Dixia, Bill Chan, Paul Yung, and Richard Kwong. My deep appreciation for their wonderful faithful work in disseminating the Uncle Reggie stories through my reggietales.org website, Facebook, YouTube, WeChat. And a special thanks to Cincinnati Children's Hospital Medical Center for "harboring me" for 47 years.

致谢

　　我非常感谢创造主给我的美好礼物：长久以来忍耐体谅我的妻子温粹英、儿子 Trevor、儿媳妇 Elaine、女儿 Olivia；我的导师，特别是布鲁斯·切斯特、保罗·布兰德和玛格丽特·布兰德、"理查德"、马克·比德尔和本·沃克；儿童医院中来自世界各地的许多研究员；特别是我亲爱的万国青年同工：诺晨光、黄瑜枫、姜维、查德·麦金托什和施凯瑞，看到他们为主所做的工作，给我很多的鼓励和喜乐。非常感谢 Jenny Liao 的热忱，开设了第一个故事网站 Reggietales.org，以及陶晴给网站更新，带来创意；还有我忠实的同工张淑贞和雷世安辛勤的工作。感谢辛城访问学者接待团队：杨华礼、Amy Zhao、Mary Fan、约翰·巴斯科姆和玛丽·安娜·卢卡斯；感谢翻译团队，他们的名字刊登于各篇文章中；还有媒体支援团队：杨迪霞、陈启源、容振威和 Richard Kwong。我深深感谢他们通过 reggietales.org 网站、脸书、视频网站 YouTube 和微信，把曾叔叔的故事传播出去。特别感谢辛辛那提儿童医院医疗中心"窝藏我"47 年。

翻译：Eileen

1. First Medical Missions Journey 1989

Since early childhood I felt the call to be involved in some way in medical missions. As time went on, even as I became more and more involved in local ministry and the academic life, the pull continued. In 1989, just prior to the June 4 incident in China, I was privileged to lead a team of 20 from Cincinnati, USA on a medical mission to southern China in an area not too far from my ancestral village. 2 weeks later, as we were leaving the beautiful farm lands, I watched the **farmers at hard work stooping** over their rice paddies. I realized that I was **looking at myself**. From that moment, I made a promise that I would return and do what I could. Over the years, indeed I was given many opportunities to bring medical teams into rural areas of China.

One year, I wrote to two organizations expressing my desire to take "early retirement" in a few years, to bring medical teams into needy areas, and whether it was of value to their work. One of the organizations basically told me to sit tight, and write them when I had my "act together". The other organization took my letter, and circulated it around for 2 years, including initially an offer to become medical director for the organization, something a newborn pediatrician was eminently not suited to do.

Little did I know then, but God was working in the hearts of two other people, Dr. Taylor and "Richard". They had just first met after a

1. 1989 年的第一次医疗援助服务

早在童年时代我就感觉到参与医疗援助服务的呼召。随着时间的流逝，即使我越来越投入参与本地的事奉和学术工作，这种呼召一直持续着。1989 年，正好是六四事件之前，我有幸带领一支由 20 人组成的医疗服务队从美国辛辛那提出发，去中国南方一个离我祖籍不远的地方。两星期后，当我们离开美丽的农村时，我看见**农民们弯着腰在稻田里费劲地做工**。我意识到我看到的是站在对边的自己。从那时刻起，我许下承诺，我要回来做我所能做的。过去许多年，我确实有许多机会带领医疗服务队进入中国的农村地区。

农田上友善的水牛
Friendly buffalo of the farmlands

23

prayer meeting at my childhood church, the Swatow Christian Church in Tsimshatsui, Hong Kong. And soon after that, my letter arrived in their hands. They prayed a silent prayer of thankfulness to God for the "coincidence".

A few months later, Dr. T **"just happened"** to be the speaker for a 1993 Midwest US retreat. We had a warm meeting in his cabin at the retreat site. Overnight, he drafted, and we discussed and concluded the first version of the beginning of MSI, Medical Services International, to serve in poverty areas of China: the "rest is history", as they say and for me, beginning a decade of meaningful and inspiring service together with Dr. T and Richard.

From the very start, my passion was to bring young people to the field, and to work with young people, which amused Dr. T to no end. During medical mission trips, I would often gravitate, like a metal chip to a magnet, towards the kids in the township middle and high schools, to teach them English. It was such a wonderful opportunity to encourage and inspire numerous young people.

One of the greatest thrills in my life is that, I have even been reconnected with some of these young people (courtesy of emails, cell phones, and text messages). They have now become part of the family, and are in medical school, nursing school, English language teacher training, computer school, and international law. In these reunions, I am thankful that the good Lord gave me a taste of what I would see, when I see Him face to face, when there will be millions of reunions. I know that even though many of the contacts we made during our many visits at many different places, were not necessarily very deep, yet I believe that, in those **"little acts of mercy and love"**, God uses those acts to touch many hearts. In most instances, we will never know the full impact in our

1. 1989 年的第一次医疗援助服务
1. First medical missions journey 1989

有一年，我写信给两个组织，表示我想在几年内"提早退休"，然后带领医疗队去有需要的地方，并问这样对他们的工作是否有帮助。其中一个组织告诉我说等等看，当我有具体行动计画时再写信给他们。另一个组织拿着我的信，转发了两年，起初更邀请我担当那个组织的医疗主任，但这工作显然**不适合**我这个新生儿科医生。

当时我不知道，神在另外两个人心里做工，这两个人就是泰勒博士和"理查德"。他们第一次见面的地方就是我童年时参与的教会——香港尖沙嘴的潮人生命堂，当时他们刚开过祷告会。不久，我的信到了他们手里。他们默默为这个"巧合"祷告感谢神。

几个月后，泰勒博士**"恰巧"**为 1993 年的美国中西部夏令营担任讲员。我们在营地他的住处中有一次温馨的会面。隔夜，我们根据他的草拟讨论并完成了计画的第一个版本，创立了国际医疗服务机构（Medical Services International, MSI），为中国的贫困地区服务——这就是 MSI 创立的历史，对我来说，这也开展了我与泰勒博士和"理查德"那十年有意义而激励人心的服务。

从一开始，我就热衷于带领年轻人到前线，跟年轻人一起工作，这一点一直让泰勒博士觉得很有趣。在医疗援助服务的旅程中，镇里的中学生经常像吸铁石一样吸引着我去教他们英语。这是一个非常好的机会，令无数年轻人得到鼓舞和激励。

我生命中令我最兴奋的其中一件事，就是能够和当中某些

lifetime, but one day we shall know.

After 10 years, I have stepped down from active duty in MSI, but I have continued this mission legacy by continuing to meet and welcome academic medical doctors from all over China, and being involved especially with young people overseas. As David Adeney, a forerunner to Dr. T., once said –and I abbreviate– "any and all ways should be our motto". It has been a remarkable journey, in which I have learned so much by being involved in medical and professional "salt and light" services, in various sites and at various levels. It is just amazing what God can do in our lives, as we are willing to be a part of that great effort.

与医疗服务的联合创始人 "理查德"、陈太太，以及中国出生的 "老华侨" 泰勒博士相聚
With co-founders of medical mission, Richard and Mrs Chen, and Dr James Taylor

1. 1989 年的第一次医疗援助服务
1. First medical missions journey 1989

年轻人继续保持联络（透过电邮、手机和短信）。他们现已成为我们信仰大家庭的成员，并且在医学院、护士学校、英语教师训练学校、电脑学校和国际法律学院就读。在这些重逢的时候，我感激主让我**预先尝到**那种滋味，就是当我与祂面对面、当我与无数人重逢时，我会看见怎样的场面。我知道即使我们去过许多不同地方、与许多人有过不太深入的接触，但我相信，神会使用那些**"怜悯和慈爱的小行动"**，感动许多人的心。在大多数情况下，我们都不知道自己的生命带来怎样的影响，但终有一天我们会知道。

　　十年后，我卸下了 MSI 的主要职责，但我仍然继续医疗援助服务的优秀传统，持续地会见并招待来自中国各地的学术医生，并且特别与海外的年轻人接触。泰勒博士的前辈大卫·艾德理曾经说（我简略为）："要用尽所有的方法，并以此为座右铭"。这是一趟出色的旅程，在旅程中，通过在不同地点和不同层次参与医疗和专业的"作盐作光"的服务，我学习到许多功课。当我们愿意成为那伟大尝试的一部分，神就会在我们的生命中作出惊人的工作。

学生常见的反应
Typical student response

翻译：张晓霓、李静

27

2. Jehovah Jireh

One of the mottos of Hudson Taylor and the China Inland Mission was "Jehovah Jireh" – the Lord provides. This is a motto adopted by my medical mission since its founding in 1994.

Soon after I announced to my somewhat surprised colleagues at the Medical School and Cincinnati Children's Hospital, that I was "stepping down" from my administrative positions to go into full time China service, I met the **Anglican Bishop**. The Bishop is the titular chairman of the Board of the Children's Hospital which is a leading institution in the US. He "congratulated' me on my decision and asked "what about the financial support for the new organization?" I had just been freshly reminded about our guiding motto, so I was very forth-right in saying - "you know, Bishop, I thought at first that I could use my vast experience in grant writing and apply for some grants. But the Lord seemed to have other ideas and work for me. I have been advised NOT to write grants. Furthermore, we are trying to adhere to a 'non-solicitation policy', so we do not really tell people about our financial needs, unless we're asked!"

The Bishop stared at me, right into my eyes. Then he grabbed me literally by the lapel and "shook" me, "**I'm asking you now!**" At this point, I "woke up" and "revealed" our lack of funds! Sure enough a few months later, a very adequate check came in the mail. Jehovah Jireh indeed.

When I had approached the Chief of the Children's Hospital and announced my intention to phase down and step out of the academic

2. 耶和华以勒

"**耶**和华以勒"在希伯来语里的意思是神必供应。这是著名的来华宣教士戴德生的座右铭之一，并且是中国内地会的使命。这也是我们的医疗服务队自 1994 年创办以来一直持守的一个座右铭。

在我向我有点吃惊的同事宣布我要辞去医学院及辛辛那提儿童医院的行政职务，打算全时间去中国服事后不久，我与美国中西部的**英国圣公会的主教**会面。那位主教是美国顶尖的辛辛那提儿童医院的董事会名誉主席。他"祝贺"我的决定，并问我新组织的资金来源。我刚好对我们的座右铭记忆犹新，所以我直截了当地说："主教，起初我想用我申请资金的丰富经验去申请资助。但主似乎有其他的主意和工作给我。我得到的建议是**不需写资金申请**。再说，我们一直试图遵守一个'不主动要求捐助的政策'。因此，除非有人问，我们一般不会告诉人我们的资金需求。"

主教盯着我的眼睛，然后他居然抓住我的翻领，"推推"我说："**我现在不是在问你吗？**"这时候，我"被点醒了"，就向他透露我们缺乏资金！果真，几个月后，一张足足够用的支票出现在邮箱里。耶和华以勒——神必供应，确实如此。

administrative leadership, I was pleasantly surprised that he took it all in stride and was most encouraging. I was shocked however when he finished our meeting and said "I assume you will need office support for this new venture", to which I said "well, that would be nice".

I had thought originally that I would need to have some office space either at home in my basement, or possibly in my home church. But I was totally unprepared for the eventual support that the Chief offered to me. Not only did I not have to ask or negotiate, I was given at first 3, then 4 and finally nearly 5 units of space; for my office, the Midwest Rep for the mission, the US and International Mobilization Secretary, a part-time (often student) helper, and a storage space. We were moved twice, but finally we were located to a self-contained 5-unit area that was private and secure, which was great for confidential discussions and prayers.

Plus we were given all necessary office support, including computers, printers, fax machines, phones, email services, engineering support and IT support, and all the opportunities within an active medical center (networking, intranet news, amenities, you name it!). This overwhelming support was topped off with direct partial financial support for staffing needs. I could literally "not believe my eyes" when the entire "package" was signed off.

Having been "raised in 'hard nosed' academia" and gone through tough "budget sessions with the Chief", accounting for every budget item and making sure every cost was covered by appropriate income, I was unprepared for this "new approach" by the Chief of the Institution. I had written no grants for this, I had made no demands, I had made no "solicitations". It was indeed a wonderful attestation of "divine intervention" – a fantastic "Jehovah Jireh" confirmation of my call to serve Him.

辛辛那提儿童医院是 1883 年由圣公会教会创立。圣公会主教是该医院董事会的名誉主席。医院的拱门提示,医院的精神是基督安慰和治疗软弱的人。

The Anglican Bishop is the titular chairman of the Board of Trustees of the Cincinnati Children's Hospital, begun in 1883 by the Anglican Church. Hospital archway is reminder of the ethos of the hospital, with Christ comforting and healing a frail lamb.

　　当我去找儿童医院的院长并慎重地告诉他我想逐渐退出学术行政领导的位子时,他从容并非常鼓励的态度让我感到惊喜。但让我震惊的是,他在结束谈话时竟然对我说:"我猜你这个新尝试会需要一个办公室。"我答道:"那当然好。"

　　我原先打算以我家的地下室或我的教会作为办公的空间。我完全没想到院长竟然会提供这样的支援。在不用我主动要求或协商的情况下,院长给了我最初三个,然后四个,最后近五

不错的办公室？
Nice office?

32

个办公空间。这就成为我、事工的中西部代表、美国及国际动员干事、兼职助手（通常是学生）的办公室，以及一个储物空间。我们搬迁了两次。最后我们迁进了一个由五个单元自成一体的地方，安全而不受打扰。这样的地方让我们可以自由谈话和祷告，是最好不过的了。

　　不仅如此，院长更供提供我们所需的一切办公设备，包括电脑、印表机、传真机、电话、电子邮件、场地维护和资讯技术支援，以及一个忙碌活跃的医疗中心应有的一切资源（如网路、内部新闻、福利设施，你能想到的我们都有！）。这些意想不到的支援还包括直接给我们职员薪资上的部分财务资助。当我在合约上签字时，我简直不敢相信自己的眼睛。

　　我在精明实际的学术界打滚多年，又体会过院长做预算时如何精打细算地确保每个预算项目和每一项开支都有对应的收入来支持，因此，医院院长的这种"新做法"让我措手不及。我没为我们的医疗服务队申请过任何资金，也没有主动要求或"讨"过任何资助。我所得到的真是一个精彩奇妙的神助的见证——奇妙的"**耶和华以勒**"确认了我被呼召去服事祂。

翻译：张晓霓、林行易

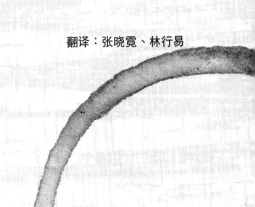

3. A Good Cancer

In my 10th year of the medical mission that I helped start in China, I was hoping to wind down my work. I had been traveling quite intensively for nearly 10 years, often 7 to 8 international trips per year, and usually staying away from home 2 to 3 weeks each time. So the toll on my family was quite serious; I had committed myself to the effort for 10 years, and felt it was time to return to serve at the Cincinnati Chinese Church, my home church. However, it was difficult to find a replacement, and so the matter kept being dragged along without clear resolution.

However in August of the 10th year, I discovered the news that I had prostate cancer. Normally a discovery like that might cause concern, but in my situation it was actually a great relief! The reason was that my father had died of prostate cancer and its spread, and so, I was always under a cloud, and knew that I would one day most likely develop the cancer also. I had been half-hoping that it would happen, so that I could get rid of it! So when the news came, I was truly quite relieved, because now, finally I could have it removed.

Also, it seemed wonderful timing, since this was my 10th year, and a good time to move on. I uttered a word of thankfulness to the Lord, and announced it cheerily to the big chief of the mission. I indicated that I would like to step down from mission leadership, and get my cancer treated. I promised the mission that, in the remaining 4 months of the year, I would try to do most of what I had planned to do in the following

3. 合时的癌症

到了我在自己有分建立的中国医疗服务队里事奉的第十年，我有了一个想要放松一下手头工作的念头。我已奔波了接近十个寒暑，每年大概出国七八次，每次离家大约两三个星期。因此我几乎顾不了家。我致力为此努力了十年，感觉到是时候回到我的母会辛城教会服事了。但是医疗服务队的事很难找人接手，这样，我想放松的念头就被拖延下来，并没有清楚的解决方案。

但是在第十年的 8 月，我发现我得了前列腺癌。这样的发现通常会让人忧虑，但是对我却是**松了一口气**！原因是我的父亲是死于前列腺癌扩散，因此我知道自己很可能也会罹患癌症，这令我一直活在阴影下。我心里有一半希望它成真，这样我就可以摆脱我内心的阴影。因此当消息传来时，我真的松了一口气，因为我现在终于可以切除它了。

再者，我感到这事发生的**时间似乎很合适**。第十年正好是我该走向人生的下一步的时候。我向主说了一句感恩的话之后便爽快地向服务队的主席宣布了这件事，并表示我想辞去我在服务队里的领导职位，去治疗癌症。我答应在剩下的四个月里，我将极尽所能将我下一年计画要做的事做完。这样我可以在来

year; so that by rushing many of the projects in the next 4 months, I could leave on January 1st, with a clear conscience. So over the next 4 months, indeed, I furiously finished off many projects.

You might think that it is odd to delay treatment for cancer, but actually I had done much reading about the disease, and had talked extensively with a wonderful prostate doctor, who answered all my relevant questions. It turns out that prostate cancer is a very slow growing cancer, and that there was really no hurry. He felt confident that delaying treatment till January was perfectly fine. So I made an appointment for early January to have it treated with radiation seeds.

Since I felt that the whole process was **providential**, I decided to use the treatment as an "excuse", and declared myself **unavailable** for any work or ministry, or even contacts with people, for 6 weeks. Actually the procedure took 90 minutes, and my recuperation was at most a few days. So I used the time in a wonderful way to commune with God, and seek direction for the next 10 years of my life. With prayer and bible study, I felt that God gave me the direction that I should focus on, and coined the vision "Youth For All Nations", marrying my twin interests of youth and missions in a vision to bring "youth of all nations" together to have a vision "**to all nations**".

Indeed, soon after the 6 weeks was over, I embarked on a renewed venture, to serve at church in youth and missions. It has been a tremendous opportunity to serve, as the youth group grew to more than 80 young people, and missions focus at CCC gradually solidified, especially in the sending and mentoring of young people to distant lands. That is another story!

Author's note: Sometimes when things that seem "bad" happen to

3. 合时的癌症
3. A Good Cancer

年1月1日安心离开。于是，在随后四个月里，我确实为此夙夜匪懈，完成了许多项目。

你可能觉得拖延治疗癌症很奇怪，但我读了许多关于这种病的资料，并跟一位出色的前列腺医生深入讨论过。他回答了我所有的问题。原来前列

水果、蔬菜和坚果总是对你有好处，或能预防癌症
Fruits, veggies and nuts are always good for you, might prevent cancer for you

腺癌是一种生长得非常慢的癌症，不需要急着治疗。他觉得将治疗过程延迟到1月是完全可行的，于是我就预定了在1月初做放射线治疗。

因为我感到这整个过程犹如**天意**，我决定以治疗为由，向大家声明我六周内将**不能**做任何工作或服事，甚至与人接触。实际上临床治疗只花了90分钟，而我最多休养了不过几天。所以我用其余的时间与神相交，为我今后十年的人生寻求指引。随着祷告和读经，我觉得神为我指出了方向，并让我看见"万国青年"的异象。这个异象结合了我对青年和宣道的热情，把"万国**的**青年"聚集起来，给他们"**到万国**事奉"的异象。

确实，过了六周后，我便马上在教会中重新开始青年和宣道两方面的事奉。在我面前的是一个极大的机会。教会的青

us, they may turn out to really be "blessings in disguise". Even prostate cancer can be a true blessing.

我六个星期的休养地点
My 6 weeks retreat

38

年小组增长至 80 多人，辛城教会的宣道重点也逐渐成型，开始差派青年人到偏远地区工作并作出指导。这又是另一个故事了！

一点感想：有时我们认为是"坏"的事情，可能会成为"伪装的祝福"，正如塞翁失马，焉知非福。即便是前列腺癌也可以是真正的祝福。

翻译：张晓霓、林行易

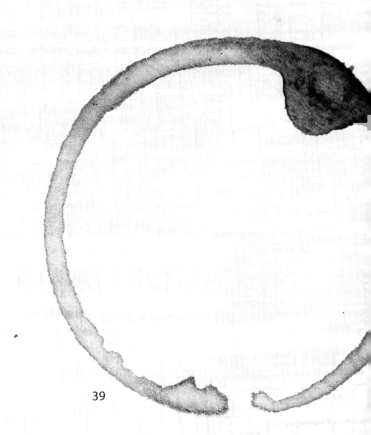

4. A Child Bride: From Boils to Matriarch

宝宝长大了，结婚后成为医院的院长夫人；感谢神给头上生疖子
The baby grows up and marries the boy that becomes the hospital director; thank God for boils

We often wonder about our mysterious ancestors. What were they thinking? Who were they? How did we come to be? We read in Genesis of the beginnings of mankind, and we are always amazed to see the dramatic display of contrasts and similarities compared with our modern lives. All life is a story, from Adam to Christ to our ancestors

4. 从疬子妹到女主人——
一个童养媳的故事

我们总会想去了解我们的神秘祖先。他们都在想什么？他们是谁？我们是怎么来的？我们看创世记中人类的起源时常常会惊叹，它和我们现代的生活有诸多相似之处，又有那么多的不同。从亚当到基督，从先祖到我们，每个生命都是一个故事。而我的梦想就是把这些故事形象地、忠实地、栩栩如生地描绘出来。

有一个女孩，出生于广东省山区一条名为五经富的小农村。小女孩刚出生的时候，她的爸爸很是失望，因为他一直想要一个男孩来传宗接代。

父亲说："快把她送人！我们不要女孩！"于是，当地一个媒婆就把这个女婴送到了别人家。

十天之后，领养的人家把媒婆叫了回来："我们不要这个孩子！她太丑了，看看她的头上，全都是疬子；赶快把她送回去吧！"

这个倒楣的媒婆只好把女婴送回那对本就不欢迎她的亲生父母那里，更糟糕的是，小女婴已经没有奶水吃了。

在回来的路上，媒婆遇到一个善良的女人，她问那个媒婆：

to us. My dream is to tell that story and stories, imaginatively, colorfully, and faithfully.

Another little girl was born in Wu King Fu ("five streets village"), a small farming village in the mountains of Guangdong Province. Dad was upset, because he needed a boy to carry the family name.

"Give her away! We don't need a girl!" father commanded. The local "mei-por", or go- between, bundled off the baby to give her to another family.

10 days later, the mei por was summoned to this family again.

"We don't want this baby! It's got a head full of boils; she's ugly, take her back where she came from!"

The poor "mei-por" had to carry the little girl, now in worse condition without her mother's milk, back towards her unwelcome home.

On the way, she met a kind woman, who asked the mei-por: "Ah por (older woman), what are you doing, going back and forth with a baby?"

After the mei-por explained the sad situation, the kind woman said, "Are you still trying to give her away? She looks very cute! I'll take her. My son will like her. She can be his bride, when they grow up!"

Indeed the baby with the boils grew up to be my grandma, who later was married to my grandpa when she was still a teenager. Grandpa became a mission hospital doctor and elder of the Wu King Fu Church, and grandpa & grandma became well respected people in the village.

One day a coolie (laborer) came to visit grandma to sell his wares. "Mei-por" happened to be in the courtyard, and told grandma "That's the person you would have married had his family kept you in his home." Grandma smiled, and thanked her newborn boils.

As the greatest book tells us, "Give thanks for everything."

(As told by cousin Au and Shiu-Mei Tsang to me, February 2000)

"阿婆，你抱着这个小女婴来来回回的在干什么呢？"

媒婆就把这个可怜小女婴的故事讲给她听，妇人听后，问道："你还想把她送人吗？她看起来真可爱！我想带她走，我的儿子肯定会喜欢她。等他们长大后，她可以做他的媳妇啊！"

你知道吗，其实这个长疖子的女婴就是我的奶奶，她在十几岁时就嫁给了我爷爷。爷爷后来成为医生，在教会医院里工作，同时也是五经富教会的长老，我的爷爷和奶奶在村子里都很受村民的爱戴。

有一天，一个肩挑竹扁担的小商贩到我奶奶家卖瓷器，媒婆碰巧也在院子里，她告诉奶奶："这是那个原先你要嫁的人，他的家人本来要把你留给他的。"奶奶笑了，真是**多亏她头上生的疖子**。

就像圣经中吩咐我们："凡事谢恩。"

（本故事由堂哥振鏀于 2000 年 2 月转述）

翻译：韩文丽、孙珺

爷爷遗像
Grandpa

5. Godly Heritage in a Mountain Village

"Heritage" is a wonderful word. In the 21st century, we are apt to think that we know it all, and history and heritage are unimportant. David in Psalm 89:1 says otherwise.

"I will sing of the LORD's great love forever; with my mouth I will make your faithfulness known through all generations." God is a faithful God and our heritage through the generations continues to impact even our 21st century lives.

Wukingfu is a small Hakka mountain village in Guangdong province, China. Grandfather was a village boy working as a "gofer" (go for this, go for that) in the Scottish Presbyterian Mission Hospital. Soon the doctors recognized that he was a bright boy and they sent him to study medicine. Grandfather became a Christian, elder of the local Hakka Church, and Superintendent of the Mission Hospital.

My father grew up in the village, but was sent to complete his high school in the British Colony of Hong Kong. There he managed to get into the University of Hong Kong Medical School, after a year or two! It had to mean that the village mission school must have been of very high quality indeed.

Soon after graduating from medical school he married my mother, an American born Chinese from Seattle who didn't even know Chinese.

5. 山中的至宝

"**传承**"是一个很宝贵的词语。在二十一世纪，我们都自以为我们了解世界，认为历史和传承对我们来说无关紧要。可是大卫，一位古代以色列的王，在诗篇八十九篇 1 节却说："我要歌唱耶和华的慈爱，直到永远；我要用口将你的信实**传与万代**。"神是信实的神，祂留给我们的产业历经万代，即使是在二十一世纪也继续影响着我们的生活。

五经富是坐落在中国广东省的一个小客家山村。我的爷爷小时候曾在村里一所属于苏格兰长老会的教会医院当一名杂役。一段日子后，医生们觉得我爷爷是个可塑之才，于是就送他去读医学院。后来，爷爷成为一名基督徒，慢慢成为了当地客家教会的长老，再后来也做了这所教会医院的院长。

我父亲也在五经富长大，后来被送到当时还是英属的香港读高中。在那里，他仅花了一年多两年的时间就考入香港大学的医学院！可见当时村里的教会学校（父亲曾在那里上学）的教学品质之高。

After graduating from the University of Washington, she had braved the Pacific to teach English in the Orient. Evidently my father's English must also have been quite good to charm her, again a "tribute" to his early mission school. During World War II my parents escaped with me as a baby into the hinterland to avoid the Japanese who had captured Hong Kong. Because my dad had a "foreign wife", they lived in the foreign doctors' quarters.

I do not remember anything about the 4 years of my early childhood in the village. But in 2000 we returned to visit the village for the first time. To my great surprise, part of the Mission Hospital was still there – and even the nurses' quarters, and the now run-down doctors' quarters where once we lived. I was reminded then that the mission had built not only the church and hospital, but also the elementary and high school, and even a bible school!

The debt we owe to those before us is often staggering. But it is easy to forget that. The tireless efforts of missionaries more than 100 years ago, and the actions of our forbears, have tremendous impact across the generations.

In 1989 when I took my first medical mission team into China, we passed by many Hakka villages not too far from my ancestral home. I saw the Hakka men and women stooping in the fields, planting the rice shoots.

As they waved to us, it dawned on me that I could have been the one stooping in the field, waving at these foreigners passing by. If the missionaries had not..., if my grandfather had not..., if my father had not....

Let us never forget the debt we owe our godly forebears, and godly men and women, ministers of the Word who traveled thousands of miles

5. 山中的至宝
5. Godly Heritage in a Mountain Village

我的客家村祖屋——青花楼
My ancestral Hakka Village
home, "Qing Hua Lou"

从医学院毕业不久，我的父亲就跟我母亲结婚了。我的母亲是在美国西雅图出生的华人，对中文一窍不通。从华盛顿大学毕业后，我的母亲毅然跨越太平洋来到东方教英语。我的母亲能被我的父亲虏获芳心，可见我父亲的英文水准也不逊色，这同样也要"归功"于他早期在教会学校求学的经验吧。在第二次世界大战期间，日本占领了香港，我的父母为了躲避日本人，带着还在襁褓中的我逃到大陆。因为我的父亲有一个"外籍妻子"，所以他们住到了外籍医生的宿舍。

我早已经忘记了在村子里那四年的童年生活。不过令我大感意外的是，在 2000 年我们第一次回到这个村子的时候，尽管时

教会医院的医生宿舍
Mission Hospital doctors' quarters

47

to take the wonderful gospel to peoples they had not previously met. Their love and dedication set in train a sequence of events that changed the world and changed each of our lives. May we never forget that, and may we in turn, be godly people who set in train a new sequence of godly traits that will last for generations to come.

福音医院旧址
The old Gospel Mission Hospital: "Fu Ying Yi Yuan"

重建后的医院名为人民医院，
大门上面架起了红色十字架
The new People's Hospital
entrance today with red cross
"Ren Min Yi Yuan" (same
hospital, reconstructed)

5. 山中的至宝
5. Godly Heritage in a Mountain Village

隔多年，当年**教会医院的部分建筑**还存留着，包括护士宿舍和我小时候住过、现已废弃的医生宿舍。我还依稀记得当时的宣教差会不仅建立了教会和医院，还有小学和高中，甚至是一所圣经学校！

随着时间的流逝，我们所受的恩惠会慢慢变得模糊，甚至被遗忘。但超过 100 年前那些宣教士无尽的努力，还有我们祖先辛勤的耕耘，却对以后的世世代代留下了深远的影响。

1989 年，我第一次带领医疗服务队去中国。我们路过好几个离我老家不远的客家村落，我看到客家人正弯着腰在稻田里**插秧**。

当他们向我挥手的时候，我忽然想到也许原本我也是他们中的一员。如果当年宣教士没有……或者如果我的爷爷没有……又或者我的父亲没有……，那么我现在也会躬耕田野，向路过的国外友人挥手。

我们绝不可忘记我们敬虔祖先留下的恩惠，还有那些敬虔的人，那些宣教士，他们不远万里来到这里并将宝贵的福音传给那些素未谋面的人。他们的爱和他们一切的奉献改变了世界，也改变了我们每个人的生命。愿我们不要忘记他们，也希望我们能以他们为榜样，成为敬虔的人并将这些敬虔的品性传承给我们的下一代。

翻译：孙珺

6. Making an Impression

It is often said that it is important to make a good impression on someone when you first meet. However, sometimes it is just important to make an impression.

One day, this 14-year-old girl arrived from Thailand. For the teenage boys in the Swatow Church Sunday school in Hong Kong, this sounded exotic. It didn't hurt that her mother showed up at times bearing gifts, such as true crocodile wallets and belts, and gold belt buckles inscribed with the royal symbol of Thailand. Apparently, these gifts were not expensive in Thailand, but to a young teenager, this smelled of exoticism.

Determined to make an impression on this cute little girl, the boys brought her innocently into our sphere of influence. So, one day "the boys" were up on a balcony on the third floor of an apartment building. We were throwing explosive "contact bombs" at unknowing passersby on the street below. We aimed the explosives just shy of the feet of the people so that they would explode and startle the unsuspecting pedestrians, while we darted away from the balcony and giggled.

Meanwhile, Esther, the Thai girl who had been sent to Hong Kong to study, began to innocently examine what we were playing with. Having never seen an explosive and being extremely meticulous and clean, she spotted a black flake on it. She used her thumbnail to scratch the flake off the bomb. The "contact" bomb instantly exploded in her hands and blew off her thumbnail completely.

6. 留下印象

人们经常说**良好**的第一印象至关重要，其实有时候，重要的只是留下**印象**。

有一天，一个 14 岁的泰国女孩来到香港的潮人生命堂。对于在教会上主日学的那些十几岁的男孩子，这是很**新奇**的事情。女孩的妈妈不时带来鳄鱼皮的钱包腰带，或者带有泰国皇族标志的黄金腰带扣等小礼物，并不会让我们有抵触心理。这些礼物在泰国不算贵重，但对于一个香港年轻人来说，却是那么的与众不同。

为了要给这个可爱的女孩留下印象，我们这些男孩子无恶意地带她来到我们的"**地盘**"。有一天，男孩子爬到了一座公寓三楼的阳台，朝下面的人行道扔摔炮。我们将这些摔炮扔在离行人还有几米的地方，爆炸的时候把不知情的行人吓一跳，而我们就会躲到阳台后面偷笑。

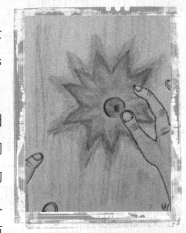

玩火——华盛顿州西雅图艺术家 Lily Heinzin 的作品
Playing with fire - a drawing by artist Lily Heinzin, Seattle, WA

In my panic and to my horror, I watched the entire off-script scenario unfold. Quickly my surgeon father appeared, and he took us angrily to his clinic, while I sheepishly accompanied the victim and tried to be as inconspicuous as possible. For weeks after that, a bandage around her thumb was a daily reminder of the traumatic event.

And up to this day, her regrown thumbnail bears the scar of the explosion. But I think the episode created a vivid impression on her, since we became childhood sweethearts and were married 10 years later, 6 days before we took off for America.

The moral of this story is that it might **not** be necessary to classify first impressions as good or bad, as long as it is an **impression**. The Good Book tells us to "remember the wife of our youth": presumably, the wife might also remember her first impression of her youthful suitor.

看，那小姑娘大拇指上的是什么？
What's on the thumb?

6. 留下印象
6. Making an Impression

与此同时,这个来香港求学的泰国女孩,开始天真地看我们在玩什么。由于她从来没见过摔炮,而她又是个注意细节和清洁的人,所以,当她在摔炮上发现了一块黑色的薄片,就想用大拇指的指甲刮下来。摔炮马上就在她手中**爆炸**了,把她的指甲完全炸了下来。

目睹整个过程的我完全吓呆了,所有人都没有预想到这件事情的发生。很快,身为外科医生的父亲来了,他大发雷霆,把我跟女孩带到他的诊所。我既紧张又害怕地伴着她,简直想找个缝钻进去。接下来的几个星期,她拇指上的绷带时时都在提醒着我那次可怕的事故。

直到今日,她的指甲上还留着爆炸时的伤疤。但是我仍觉得这一幕给她留下了深刻的印象,因为后来我们就成了青梅竹马的恋人,十年后,也就是我们前往美国的六天前,我们结为了夫妻。

这个故事的意义在于,**没有**必要过于在意第一印象的好坏,只要留下**印象**就好。圣经吩咐我们:"要记念(和合本作:喜悦)你幼年所娶的妻",妻子大概也会记得她对那个年轻求婚者的第一印象。

翻译:韩文丽、孙珺

7. Burning Down the House

It is amazing how many times in life we have a narrow escape from tragedy, but we often easily forget.

As a teenager, I had a fascination with fire. I had a trick where I soaked cotton balls in alcohol, lit them, and then threw them up in the air as fireballs without burning myself. (Reader, beware. Don't attempt this at home!) The premise was that the flame burned only upwards and not downwards, or at least that was the theory. In one of my antics at home, throwing a bunch of flaming cotton balls into the air, I missed catching them and they fell to the floor, instantaneously morphing into more than 20 small balls of fire that raced on the wooden floor in different directions, including towards my father's medical clinic attached to our home. Needless to say, Dad was not at all amused. Burning down the house and clinic was not an endearing idea.

As a young fellow in medical research, I remember thinking of a bright idea to flush out my pipettes in the lab. There were few fancy machines then, so I thought I could design one. I used running water to create a vacuum effect, sucking up water through the pipettes and therefore rinsing them continuously without the need for manual action—that is, by me. Leaving this contraption for longer and longer periods without mishap, I became bolder, so I decided to let it run overnight to really clean the pipettes.

7. 烧毁家园

不要玩火
Don't play with fire

让人惊奇的是，我们总是轻易忘记在我们身上有多少次险些发生悲剧。

我青少年时对火十分着迷。我有一个不会伤害自己的小把戏，就是把很多棉球蘸上酒精，然后点燃它们扔向空中，就如同扔出很多个火球一样。（读者要注意：请勿在家中模仿。）当时的我知道这个小把戏能成功的原理是火焰只会向上烧，而不会向下烧。有一次，我在家中玩这个小把戏的时候，我没有接住几个燃烧着的小棉球，于是这些落在木地板上的小棉球瞬

To my horror the next morning, the lab had flooded. Plus, the water had soaked down to the floor below, dripping onto the grant that was being written by the director of the institution. I dared not show up for weeks after that. Flooding your research institution at least is not fatal, though I suspect it could alter one's research career.

One day we were driving from Cincinnati to a retreat in New York. One of my young relatives was in charge of the driving. I was sitting in the danger seat in the front. However, I fell asleep. I woke up as I saw the car flying through the air and off the expressway. I could see my life flashing before me, and I surmised that this was how it would end. I muttered a prayer like "Lord, I'm coming home."

To my total surprise, the car landed in a side ditch below the expressway, turned 180 degrees from the original direction. Somehow we landed next to a fence, and the police had to come by and drag us out of the ditch, all unharmed—miraculous, I thought. Some special angel was working overtime.

Not too long ago, I was driving from my home to the hospital one morning. A minute later and just up the street from where we lived, there was a turn in the road. My trusty black bag was lodged between the two seats in the front. Somehow, at the turn, I sensed the bag was slipping backwards. Instinctively I grabbed the black bag, and I guess I took my eyes off the street for a split second, right at the turn; or possibly I

我那辆车头被撞成 V 字型的车
My V-shaped car

间变成 20 多个小火球并向不同方向乱窜，包括窜向父亲那所与房子相连的诊所。父亲理所应当地不觉得这是件好笑的事情。烧掉房子跟诊所并不是一个好主意。

我记得当我还是个年轻的医学研究员时，我有一个洗试管的好主意。当时的实验室里几乎没有什么豪华的设备，所以我以为我可以设计一个。我用流动的水制造了一个吸力的效果，不需要用人手操作就能把水吸出来让试管被反复洗刷——重点是不用我去操作。任由这个神奇的装置长时间运行而没有发生事故后，我变得大胆起来，我决定让这个机器通宵运作，把试管彻底洗净。

让我震惊的是第二天早上整个实验室都淹了。再加上水渗透了地板，滴到了楼下研究所主管所写的专案拨款建议上。之后的几周我都不敢在研究所出现。虽然把研究所给淹了不致危害人命，但是我认为这能影响一个人的研究生涯。

有一天，我们从辛辛那提驾车前往纽约参加退修会。我一个年轻的亲戚负责开车，我就坐在司机旁的座位。但是，我睡着了。醒来的时候我看到车子在半空中飞出了高速公路。我能看到我的一生闪现在我眼前，然后我猜这就是我人生的终结了。我模模糊糊地祷告，貌似说着："主啊，我要来天家啦。"

让我非常意外的是，车子在横向旋转了 180 度之后在公路底下的沟里着陆。不知怎的，我们在围栏旁边着陆了，要警员过来把我们从沟里拉出去，但我们却奇迹般毫发无损。必定是有些特别的天使在加班工作。

stepped on the gas pedal by accident.

Suddenly, without any warning, I smashed into a very solid telephone pole. It felt like hitting solid rock. I could feel the sudden thud at the front of my car, which was spliced into a V shape.

The automatic air bag exploded from the impact-triggered chemical reaction, and chemicals shot over my neck. My body strap instantly tightened and burned into my neck and chest. Intense smoke filled inside the car, and I quickly climbed out, assuming a fire or explosion would be coming at any second.

Nothing much more happened, however, than the abrasions, but I was in a daze. The policeman arrived and sized me up. He was not in a good humor and even gave me a ticket for running into a telephone pole. Hmmm. At least I was alive.

There are close encounters in life that we easily forget and move on from, but "what if . . ." comes to mind. Yes, indeed, what if? And what happens next if "what if" does happen? Have we thought carefully about what might be next? Hmmm.

因为化学物质与安全带而留下的伤疤
Chemical and safety strap marks

58

7. 烧毁家园
7. Burning Down the House

不久前的一个早上，我开车从家里出发到医院。只一分钟车程，就到了我们住的街上的一个转弯口。我经常带着的那个黑色包包被放在前座两个座位之间。不知怎的，在拐弯的时候我发觉那个包包在向后滑。我马上抓住了那个包包，我猜在拐弯的时候我有一刹那没有注意到路面的情况；还是我可能意外地踩了油门？

突然，在我完全没有警觉的情况下，我撞向一根非常结实的电话线杆。这感觉就像是撞上了一块硬石头。我能感觉到从车头传来轰的一下撞击声，然后车头被撞成了 V 字型。

自动气囊因为撞击弹出并触发了化学反应，那些化学物质溅向我的脖子。我的安全带迅速拉紧并且磨损了我的脖子和胸口。车子内立刻充满烟雾，我怕车子会随时起火或者爆炸，所以马上爬出车外。

除了擦伤之外并无大碍，但是我觉得晕乎乎的。接着警员就到了，并且上下打量着我。他心情不是太好，甚至给我开了一张撞电话线杆的罚单。唔，至少我还活着。

人生中有些经历是我们很容易就忘记，就迈过去的，但是脑海中会浮现"如果……又如何"的想法。对，就是如果。如果真的出现了"如果"，那又会发生什么事呢？我们可有认真地想过接下来会发生什么事？唔……

翻译：孙珺

8. The Guru and Teachability

我的个人导师 "理查德"
Richard, my personal guru

One of my most impressive mentors has been "Richard." I like to call him my guru, which is just another word for a master/mentor/teacher. I could literally sit for hours listening to him talk. He had a rather rambling style of talk, so if I was not paying attention, I might miss some of his pearls of wisdom. Often he would digress and give a story, but if I paid enough attention, there was usually a moral to the story, a pearl to be gleaned from his vast experience.

As a young man, he had wandered from his faith. He had made very good money and was running several productive factories. One day he decided to give a factory to one of his daughters. He tried to "bribe her" (his words) to take the job, with a gift of a new car. That day they were driving

8. 导师与受教的心

"**理查德**"是对我影响最大的导师之一。我喜欢称呼他为我的 guru，这是老师、导师、引路人的另一种说法。我真的可以坐下来听他说上几个小时的话。他讲话的时候话题非常跳跃发散，所以如果我不认真地听，很可能会错过他话语中的"瑰宝"。他经常会岔开主题而讲一个故事，但是如果我够专心的话，通常都能发现故事中的教训，从他丰富的经验中收集到宝贵的"珍珠"。

年轻时的他曾偏离信仰。他赚了许多钱，经营几间效益很好的工厂。有一天，他决定把一间工厂送给他其中一个女儿。他尝试送她一辆新车，以"贿赂"（这是他使用的字眼）他的女儿去接受这份工作。那天他们开到加州的沙漠去试新车。后来，新车抛锚了，在等待援助的时候，理查德走进了沙漠去散步。

在沙漠中，他脑海里浮现出圣经里出埃及记的故事。他感觉到一把声音很清晰地用英语叫他："理查德，回家吧。"就在接下来的周末，他又重回教会，也回归了他的信仰，并且从那一刻起从未离开过。最后他发现，原来在他远离信仰的那些年间，他的母亲一直不断为他的回归而祷告。

out to the California desert to try out the new car. However, the new car stalled, and while they waited for help, Richard wandered into the desert.

There in the desert, he visualized the biblical exodus story. He felt he distinctly heard a voice calling to him in English: "Richard, come home." The following weekend, he returned to church and his faith, which he never left again. It turned out that his mother had been praying for him to do just that throughout all his wandering years.

With his extensive business connections at a time when the Chinese economy was a great mystery to the outside world, things began to happen for Richard. He had many former classmates and friends from Yenching University, the top university in China, which was later incorporated into Beijing University. Many of his schoolmates became party leaders and were in charge of important divisions of government. With patriotism burning for his motherland, he hosted an exhibition in New York for Americans to understand the vast economy and opportunities that were in China. This was the first big New China exhibition ever on American soil. He garnered a fantastic reputation, which included many contacts among American legislators and Chinese businessman. At this exhibition, new Chinese products were first exposed to US entrepreneurs, and the rest is history.

But Richard was not satisfied. With his refound faith, he wanted to serve God in a better way, and soon the opportunities came, as many who wanted to help in China began to show up at his doorstep. Richard had an ailment that got progressively worse, which made travel rather difficult for him. In spite of this, he traveled extensively until he could no longer travel well. He met many high-level officials, and he smoothed the path for many organizations. What was amazing was that after he had made the initial face-to-face encounter, he would spend hours and hours, day

当时很多国家都不了解中国的经济情况，但由于他在中美之间有频繁的生意往来，对他来说情况开始转变。他有许多燕京大学的老同学与朋友，燕京大学是当时最好的大学，后来合并成了北京大学。他有许多校友后来成为了党领导人或者是重要的政府官员。出于对祖国的热忱，他在纽约主办了一个展览会，以宣传中国庞大的经济体系与机遇。这是在美国本土举办的第一次大型的新中国展览会。他借此获得了无与伦比的名声，同时也结交了许多美国立法者与中国商人。在这次展览会上，新中国的产品第一次展现在美国企业家面前，之后的就是历史的见证了。

但是理查德并没有就此满足。重拾信仰的他希望能更好地服事神，而机会很快就来了，有很多希望能在中国帮点忙的人都来找他。理查德原本的小毛病开始越发严重，甚至是外出旅行亦变得艰难。然而他并没有理会，反而到处旅行直到他很勉强地完成行程。他会见了很多高层政府官员，也为很多机构铺平了道路。让人惊奇不已的是，在第一次面对面交流之后，他都会花上许多时间以电话来与人沟通，而且他认为这种联络方式同样有效。

他在香港的家很快成为了他的办公室，从世界各地来的人都去他的家与他会面。到访的人都会在理查德的客厅里围着坐，逐一等候他提供贤明之见。他的话总是一语中的。我还记得我带着一些机构的代表去到他家里听他的意见。接受了他的意见之后，事情总是很顺利。若不接受他的意见，事情总是会往不好的方向

and night, on the phone, which he said was just as effective.

His Hong Kong home became his office, and people from all over the world would fly into his home and meet him there. Sitting in a circle in his living room, everyone would wait for Richard to give his sage advice. His advice seemed always right on the spot. I remember bringing delegations to his home to hear him. When we took his advice, things went well. When we did not take his advice, things went badly. I remember him telling me how one organization had an extremely difficult time and was even thrown out of China, and how he gave them excellent advice so that they could reenter China through a very different way. "Don't get too big," he would say: "*Shu da jao feng*—Big tree attracts wind."

Through all of this, I learned the principle of teachability. As we sat there as teachable students of the guru, we learned to be quiet when we needed to be quiet and to listen to the teacher teach. I remember bringing one young aggressive director to meet him. This individual decided that it would be good to tell Richard about all the problems and all the solutions, and on and on it went. Richard sat there and said nothing. At the very end of this lengthy monologue, Richard thanked us, and we went our way. My friend asked me, "How come he didn't say anything?" to which, I replied, "Because you were talking." There was dead silence.

To be teachable means learning to shut one's mouth and to listen. In this world, we are often taught to be aggressive, to talk and talk and express all the wonderful ideas that we have. Teachability means that we have a teachable heart, that we are willing to listen to the teacher.

I often go to China or northern Thailand to teach young children and youth in remote mountain areas. What often impresses me is their teachable spirit. These kids in rural areas especially have a great respect for teachers, and they respond in wonderful ways. You can see the sparkle

发展。我记得他告诉我，曾经有一个机构捱尽苦头，甚至被赶出中国，然后他告诉他们怎样以一种截然不同的方式重新进入中国。他总是说："不要发展得过大，因为树大招风。"

这一切让我学会了要有一颗受教的心。当我们像"孺子"一样坐在导师面前时，我们学会了在需要安静的时候保持安静，在需要聆听老师教导的时候认真聆听。我记得曾经带着一位非常固执己见的年轻主任去见理查德。这个人认为应该把所有问题和所有解决方式都对理查德说一遍，于是他不断地说啊说。理查德只是坐着，什么也没说。在听完这些长篇大论的自说自话之后，理查德向我们道谢，我们就离开了。我的朋友问我："他怎么能什么都不说呢？"我回答说："因为你一直在说话啊。"然后我们都陷入了沉默。

要有受教的心意味着学会闭上自己的嘴去聆听。在这个世界，我们所受的教导往往是要善于表现自己，不断地说话以表达自己所有的好主意。有一颗受教的心，意味着我们愿意去听老师的教导。

我经常去中国或者泰国北部偏远的山区教导孩子与年轻人。让我印象深刻的是他们都有一颗受教的心。乡村地区的这些孩子特别尊敬老师，他们的反应也是可圈可点的。你能看到他们注视老师时候眼睛里的那一种火花。他们注意力非常集中，非常渴望学习。你真的能看见这些孩子在学习中透露出单纯的快乐。这就是为什么当我带着医疗队伍来到这些地区时，相比于在诊所里工作，队伍中的医生和护士更喜欢在学校教书。这

in their eyes as they focus their attention totally on the teacher. They are very attentive, and they want to learn. You can truly see the pure joy of learning in these kids. That's why when I brought medical teams into these areas, the doctors and nurses preferred to teach in the schools rather than work in the clinics. The attraction was so great that our own administration put the brakes on and warned us not to overdo it.

I realized that people who are teachable can learn a lot. The spirit of teachability is something that we in the West sometimes forget, to our detriment. When Christ said that to enter into the kingdom of heaven, we have to be as children, I think He meant that we have to be teachable; we have to have the humblest of heart and attitude and be willing to sit before the Master and listen to Him tell us, teach us, and inspire us.

I have had many mentees myself, both in the academic and spiritual realm. There's little question to me that those who remained teachable blossomed and grew to be the wonderful people that they are. One academic fellow would basically barge into my office at 5:00 p.m. nearly every day and insist on "draining my brain." He would provoke me to talk through case scenarios, academic puzzles, research dilemmas, and faith-related questions, and we would spend the next hour in wonderful debate. I could feel my brain draining out to him. It was intense, but invigorating. Other young people have been willing to sit down with me over a meal or to talk to me on the phone just to chat or to ask about directions in life, or the decisions that have to be made.

May all of us maintain that spirit of teachability and learn from teachers, mentors, and yes, even gurus.

8. 导师与受教的心
8. The Guru and Teachability

种吸引力是那么大，以致我们的行政部常常提醒我们不要忘记自己的本职，尽量少去做教书的工作。

我发现受教的人能学到更多东西。这种受教的心在西方经常被遗忘，这实在是我们的损失。基督说进入天国的人都要像孩子一样，我想祂的意思应该是要我们有受教的心。我们要有谦卑的心与谦卑的态度，愿意在主面前坐下来，认真地听祂，让祂吩咐、教导和启发我们。

在学术上与灵命上，我都有许多后辈。那些一直存有受教之心的人毫无疑问都成为了非常优秀的人。有一个研究生基本上每天下午5时都会冲进我的办公室，坚持"榨干我的脑细胞"。他通过各种案例、学术上的难题、研究上的困境和信仰上的问题来鼓励我表达自己，然后我们会花一小时作出精彩的讨论。我能感觉到我的脑汁都要被他榨干了。这个过程非常激烈，但是让人精力充沛。另一些年轻人就希望用一顿饭的时间或者通过电话来与我聊天，或是为人生的方向，或是为要做的决定寻求指引。

盼望我们每个人都有一颗受教的心，向老师、导师，甚至 *guru* 学习。

翻译：孙珺

受教、好学的学生
Teachable, wildly enthusiastic school kids

9. A Kyphosis Story

Kyphosis is a condition where the spine is deformed, commonly called "hunchback". In story books we often hear how some people are quite mean to "hunchbacks". But Tian (Providence) has a way of changing one's life from deformity to significance.

I met Sherrie many years ago as part of our mission to small towns in China. Her family was very poor. Her mother was an extremely capable farmer who had eloped with her blind husband-to-be. The blind man had been helping around in their home, and she took a fancy and compassion for him. Against all advice, she ran away with him. She decided also, that as a blind person, he would particularly be excited to have lots of children, and so, in spite of the fact there was clearly a government ban on more than one child, she decided to have 4 children! To have 4 children at that time in China (and even now) was totally unheard of, and she suffered greatly for that.

In fact, she said that when her second child was born, the nursing staff warned her that the child could be put to death, unless she immediately took the child and ran away, which she did. Whether it is true that they would have done so or not, we will never know, but she remembers it that way. With her subsequent children being born out of the law, the local officials decided to teach her a lesson. Her whole home was ransacked (*cao jia*), all of her belongings were dumped on the roadside, and her home

9. 直起腰来的故事

脊柱后凸症是一种脊柱变形而产生的情况，俗称驼背。在故事书里，我们常看到驼背的人受到十分刻薄的对待。但是，老天总是有方法把一个人残缺的人生改变成为精彩的人生。

我在很多年前返回中国支援乡村的时候遇到了雪丽。她的家很穷，她妈妈是一位非常能干的农民，她爸爸是瞎眼的，当初在她妈妈家中打工。妈妈对他又爱又怜，于是不顾一切与他私奔。她认为瞎眼的丈夫会希望有很多孩子，所以，即使政府只允许生一个孩子，她也决定要为他生四个孩子！养育四个孩子在当时的中国（甚至现在）几乎是一件闻所未闻的事情，她也为此受了很多苦。

事实上，她说在她的第二个孩子出生时，护士就警告过她这个孩子可能会被处死，除非她马上带着孩子逃跑，于是她就照做了。我们永远也不知道他们是不是真的会处死那个孩子，但是至少这是她的想法。在她随后的孩子非法出生后，当地官员决定给她点儿颜色看看。她被抄家了，所有财产都被扔在路旁，房子也被封了。邻居朝她和家人丢石头，而她相信雪丽的背就是这么被石头打坏了。

barricaded. The neighbors threw rocks at the family, and she claimed that it was one of those rocks that broke Sherrie's back.

We will never know the exact details, but from a medical viewpoint Sherrie's kyphosis seemed be a congenital defect. Our medical team were very concerned and, out of compassion, raised enough funds for an operation. However on examining the X-rays, our US Orthopedics experts counseled against it, because he felt there were not adequate resources and local expertise for such a very difficult operation at the time.

During her travails, the mother actually went to Beijing, and staged a one person sit-in at the Department of Justice. For months, she sat there with her children, but to no avail, and in spite of repeated appeals, she had to return home. At home, there was a small space for all the family to live together, behind a curtain. In the narrow so called "living area", there was only a stove and a small bench-like table for meals. The mother went off to the farm during daytime, and came back in the afternoon carrying her vegetables. This she did for years to support her husband, and 4 children to grow up and attend school.

Every 6 months, our team came to town, and we always visited with the family. They were a lovely family, and it was wonderful to be with them. Felicia (the second child) and Linda (the third) especially loved to talk with us. They practiced their English on us, and after we left, they practiced on each other. Their English became excellent, and after high school, Linda went on to teachers' college in another province, Henan, returning to teach English at her home school! Felicia went on to study nursing in Kunming, returning to her hometown also to serve! Willis, the youngest one, always very timid, grew up quickly at vocational school, mastering computer skills, and is a fine mature young man now.

After high school, Sherrie (the oldest) studied horticulture in

　　我们不可能知道当时的具体情况，但是从医学角度来说，雪丽的驼背像是先天不足所致。出于怜悯，我们的医疗队筹到足够的款项来为雪丽做手术。但是在做完 X 光检查后，我们的整形外科专家却反对做这个手术，因为他认为当时我们并没有足够的医疗资源和本地的专家来做一个这么复杂的手术。

雪丽在 XD 美好而温馨的家：琳达、威利斯、费利西亚和他们的父母
Sherrie's wonderful and warm home in XD: Linda, Willis, Felicia, parents

　　在这些事情发生的时候，她的妈妈其实到过北京，并且到司法部进行一人抗议。她跟孩子在那里呆了几个月，但毫无结果。虽然反复上诉，最后却仍被遣送回家。在家中，整家人只有在帘子后面一个很小的生活空间。在那个狭窄的生活区域，他们只有一个炉子和一个板凳一样的桌子，用来吃饭。母亲白天去干农活，傍晚才带着蔬菜回来。她就是这样养活了丈夫和四个孩子，并且供书教学。

　　每隔六个月，我们医疗队来到镇上的时候，都会去拜访他们一家。他们这一家非常温馨，每次跟他们在一起的时刻都很美好。家里的费利西亚（老二）和琳达（老三）特别喜欢跟我们聊天。她们跟我们练习英语口语，等我们走了以后，她们就互相练习。她们英语越来越好，琳达在高中毕业之后进了河南

Kunming. Later she worked in computer sales, to help support her family. In Kunming, she was encouraged by mission friends. Her faith deepened, and her attitude towards life became an inspiration to others. She developed a website that attracted more than 1,000 members, to raise money to help support poor village people. Periodically, she brought gifts to villagers in the mountains, especially during periods of local disasters, such as the great drought in Yunnan. Often, she and her friends delivered bottles of clean water to the thirsty mountain folk.

许多朋友和雪丽（穿红衣的）一起来 KM 酒店深望我

Many friends come with Sherrie, in red, to visit me at the KM hotel

During this web based venture, Sherrie met a prominent local orthopedic surgeon, who decided to operate on her. He was very impressed that she was the **mastermind** behind the web-based charity, and decided to charge an extremely low fee. Her blog friends kept up the public blog for her, with a daily "blow by blow" account of her operation, which created a sensation in Kunming, and enhanced the good name of the doctor. Her operation was quite successful, and today her back looks nearly normal.

Comment: Providential meetings, encouragements and inspiration have all been part of this story of kyphosis. Today, when you see Sherrie, you would not even realize that she had kyphosis. Her kyphosis has been corrected externally and internally, and she regularly loves to give praises and thanks to her Creator.

的师范院校，最后回到家乡的学校担任英语老师！费利西亚去昆明学习护理专业，最后也回到家乡服务。年纪最小的威利斯非常内向，他在职业学校里进步神速，很快就掌握了电脑的技能，现在已经是一个成熟的年轻人了。

高中毕业后，雪丽（老大）在昆明学习园艺，后来从事销售电脑的工作来帮补家计。在昆明，她得到一些宣教士朋友的鼓励。她的信心加深了，对生活的态度也逐渐影响着周围的朋友。她开发了一个帮助穷苦村庄人民筹款的网站，吸引了超过1,000 名会员。每隔一段时间，她都会把礼物带给山里的村民，特别是发生了如云南大旱等重大灾难的时候。她和朋友又常常把瓶装水带给山里需要干净水的村民。

就在雪丽做那个网站项目的时候，她遇到了当地一个杰出的整形外科医生，这个医生决定为她做手术。当他知道雪丽是这个网站慈善组织的**主创人**时，他深受感动，所以决定只收取非常低的手术费用。博客上的朋友帮她更新她的博客，每天都更新她手术的进展，这一系列博文在昆明造成了很大的轰动，也为这位医生带来了好名声。她的手术十分成功，并且她的背现在已经与正常人无异了。

一点感想：天意安排的会面、激励与鼓舞都是这个驼背故事的一部分。如果你今天见到雪丽，你甚至不会认为她曾经是驼背。她的驼背内外都已经矫正了，她也经常赞美以及感谢她的创造者。

翻译：韩文丽、孙珺

10. Lucy Diana, the Childhood Party Secretary

露西·戴安娜，右一
Lucy Diana, first on right

From the very beginning of our work in the small town of LQ, we met Diana, who at that time we called Lucy. Lucy Diana was a daughter of a nurse in the hospital that we had befriended. The nurse brought Lucy Diana to lunch one day, and I had a chance to chat with her. I found her to be a really engaging and lively 12-year-old, who was not shy at all to speak to a foreigner. I took her on a walk around town, where I tried to teach her simple English for different objects, like car, house, etc. She also regaled me with little bits of gossip about the local dignitaries, how this person had several wives, and that other person had a car (unusual in those days), etc. The walk around the town lasted only

10. 露西·戴安娜——
儿童版的党书记

我们一开始在禄劝这个小镇上工作时，就遇见戴安娜，那时候我们叫她露西。露西·戴安娜是我们在医院认识的一位护士的女儿。某日，那位护士在午餐时把露西带来医院，因此我有机会与她聊天。我发现她是个逗人喜爱、活泼的 12 岁女孩，和我这个"外国人"说话时一点也不害羞。我带她到镇上溜达，尝试教她用简单的英语说出东西的名称，如汽车、房子等等。她亦逗我开心，细数当地显赫人士的秘密，例如某某人如何娶得数个太太，某某人有一部汽车（在当时很不寻常）等等。因为我们得离开那儿到别的地方去，所以在镇上散步的时间只有一个小时左右，然而我们之间深厚的友谊就此萌芽。

六个月后，我们又回到这个镇上，这一次，午餐时间露西自己跑来了。她抓住我的手，坚持要我到她的学校教英语。我拒绝了，说那是不可能的，因为我是医疗队的成员，我们不是官方批准来这里当英语老师的。然而，露西不接受"不"这个答案，她握着我的手，拖着我来到她老师的家。

在中国，小镇的老师通常住在学校附近，学生们也知道老

about an hour, since we had to leave, but it began a deep friendship.

6 months later, we were back in the same town, and this time Lucy Diana came to lunch herself. Grabbing hold of my hand, she insisted that I should go and teach English at her school. I declined, and said that was not possible, since I was a member of a medical team and we were not **officially** here as English teachers. However, Lucy would not take "no" for an answer, and literally she held me by the hand, and dragged me along to the home of her teacher.

The teachers in small towns usually live close to the school, and the kids know where the teachers live. Lucy knocked on the door of her teacher, and introduced me as a friend who came from America, and "who could teach English". In her inimitable way she said to the teacher, "you want him to speak in our class, right?" The teacher sized me up and chatted with me for 2 or 3 minutes; when he recognized me as leading the medical team, he said, "Why not? Let's go, it's time for class anyway."

And so in short order, we were at his class, which was just beginning. He walked me into the room and introduced me to the class, announcing: "Today, we have a special event, we have a friend from America, and he's going to teach English." The classroom cheered, and the teacher sat down in the back of the room, but **disappeared** after a few minutes. I was left alone with the class, so I gamely introduced myself and started teaching. It was such great fun and the response was fantastic.

Half way through the class, the next classroom teacher came by and waved at me, and I said, "*Ganma* (what's up)?" She whispered to me, "After you're done with your class, come over and teach my class?" I quickly agreed. So within the next 3 days, I taught 7 classes in English, and the rest is history.

From this day, I calculated that our teams were able to teach 10,000

10. 露西·戴安娜——儿童版的党书记
10. Lucy Diana, the Childhood Party Secretary

师住在哪里。露西敲了敲老师的家门，然后介绍我是来自美国的朋友，是"那个会教英语的人"。她用谁都模仿不了的独特神态对老师说："你要他来我们班上讲话，对不对？"老师打量我一下，然后与我聊了两三分钟；知道我就是医疗队的领导后，他说："有何不可呢？走吧，反正该上课了。"

于是，我们很快就来到他的教室，那时候学生正好要上课。他陪我进教室，把我介绍给班上同学，然后宣布："我们今天有特别的安排。有一位来自美国的朋友要教我们说英语。"学生们一阵欢呼，老师就在教室后面坐下，但几分钟之后他却**消失**了。班上只留下我和一班学生，我壮着胆子介绍自己，然后开始教学。我教得很开心，学生的反应也出奇地好。

课上了一半的时候，隔壁班的老师跑过来向我招手，我说："干吗？"她压低声音问："你教完这一班，就过来教我的班？"我立刻就同意了。接下来那几天，我教了七班英语课。这次的教学经验，开启了往后我们在这个地区的英语教学服务工作。

我计算过，我们医疗队在那几年一共教了不下一万个教学时数。比如说，有一个晚上，由教师组成的代表团来到我们下榻的旅馆见我们。老师们邀请我们整个医疗队当晚去教英语。

我们共十个人来到学校。我们算过，我们可以教五班，每班有两个老师。但是校长把老师们叫到一边，然后回来，大声说："这太完美了！你们有十位老师，因此我们可以**把全校**分成十班；也就是每两班合成一班，每班 130 名学生。从七点半到十点，你们有一整晚的时间教他们。"

student hours over the next few years. For example, one evening, a teacher delegation came to the hostel to meet us. The teachers requested that we bring our entire team to teach English that evening.

We arrived at the school with 10 people. We figured that we would try to teach 5 classes, with 2 teachers in each class. However the principal huddled together with the teachers, came back, and exclaimed to us, "This is perfect! You have 10 teachers, and so we will combine the entire school into 10 classes; each classroom will have 130 kids, a combination of 2 classes into 1, and you can have the whole night to teach them, from 7:30 to 10:00 pm."

I turned to my team, some of whom had turned pale. One of them exclaimed: "I never taught a class!" and so I gave the the encouragement: "Don't worry, God will be with you." So each one of us was now sent into each "lions den". I personally escorted each teacher to each room, and gently shoved him/her in, bidding "Godspeed". That night, indeed we had all 1,300 students, and it was just "heaven" to all of us, to be able to teach so many young kids.

After that experience, the team was on cloud 9, and could barely escape from the attention and throngs that now came around us, whenever we met "the kids" on the streets of the town.

It turned out that some teachers in XD, another town in the province, soon heard about what was happening at LQ, only a few hours away. They got all excited, and started inviting our medical team at XD to teach also. So Lucy Diana is credibly the origin of the English teaching at both of these towns. We joked that Lucy Diana would be the future "party secretary" of the town, because of her obvious leadership skills. Actually, as demonstration of leadership, it was quite common that she would come up to us, followed by a group of 8 or 9, mostly boys, and would give

我回头看我的团队，有的人脸色发青。其中一人说："我**从来没教过书啊！**"因此我鼓励他们说："不要担心，神与你们同在！"我们每个人就这样一个一个被送进"虎穴"。我亲自把老师们送到各自的教室，轻轻的推他们进教室，并鼓励他们："神的恩典与你同在"。那天晚上我们有 1,300 名学生，对我们来说，能够教那么多小朋友，感觉简直就像是在"天堂"一样。

那次经验以后，我们这一队经常感觉飘飘欲仙，走在街上很难不引起群众的注意，每每在街上遇见那些"学童"，他们总会围着我们转。

结果寻甸镇的一些老师不久就听到在禄劝镇发生的事情，寻甸与禄劝位于同一个省里，两镇相距有数小时车程，镇上的老师十分兴奋，开始邀请医疗队到寻甸镇去教英文。无可质疑的是，露西·戴安娜是这两个城镇英语教学的始祖。我们开玩笑说，由于露西·戴安娜的领导能力有目共睹，我们估计她将是这个城镇未来的党书记。事实上，从一些事就可看出她的领导力：她时常自动找上我们，而背后总尾随了八九名通常是男孩子的一群人，然后提出很明确的请求，通常是："**我们邀请您于某日某时到某教室教学**"，或"**我们本周六去爬山吧**"。

从上课的安排看，这些小学生好像享有不少自由，而且有领导"权威"。他们通常会在**路上拦住我们**，邀请我们到学校去，给我们时间、地点等详细的资料。有时候，我们会婉拒他们说："不行，不行，我们没办法做到。"但是他们会说："没

us specific requests. It was usually like, "**we would like you** to teach at a certain time, and at a certain class", or "**let's go** mountain climbing this Saturday".

The way that the school classes were organized, it seemed that the kids had quite a bit of freedom and leadership "authority". They would often literally **accost us** on the streets and invite us to the school, giving us exact specifications about what time, and what class. We would remonstrate and say, "no, no, we can't do that." But they would say, "It's ok, we've already checked with the teacher, and she said fine, as long as we could convince the 'laowai' (foreigners), they can come." And when we arrived in the school, sure enough, the kids had already arranged the classes that we would teach. It was such a great experience!

Lucy Diana would often take us on mountain hikes, and you could see her leadership skills clearly. At a fork in the road, she would often turn and poll the kids following her about which way to go; however, even though a number of kids might say we should go to the **left**, she would size it up, and then she would turn around to us and say confidently, "We are going to the **right side**." Clearly a demonstration of her ability to **inspire** a following, including us, and make decisions!

It is not really a surprise, I suppose, that we now find that she graduated from medical school in 2009 and is now an anesthesia doctor in a small Yunnan town! We trust that God will continue to guide her in her steps ahead. A seed sown, and a fruit which we hope will lead to many other fruits!

Author's comments: It is a real joy and pleasure to work with young people, to observe the talents that Providence has given them, and to see them grow up to serve others, whether they are party secretaries or not!

关系的，我们已经跟老师确认过了，她说只要我们有办法说服你们老外，你们就可以来。"当我们来到学校，的确，学生们已经组织好班级让我们教。那是一次非常棒的体验。

露西·戴安娜常常带我们去爬山，在这时候就可以清楚看出她的领导能力。到了分叉路口时，她会转身问同伴该走哪个方向；不过，即使有不少同伴都说该走**左边**，经过仔细估量以后，她会转向我们，然后自信地说："我

爬山活动（左三就是露西·戴安娜）
Mountain hiking (Lucy Diana is third from left)

们走**右边**。"她真的具有**激发**群众的能力，包括我们，然后作出决定！

因此，当我们发现她已经于 2009 年自医学院毕业，现在在云南某一个小镇当麻醉科医师时，真的一点都不惊讶。我们坚信神会继续引领她前面的脚步。种子已经播了，我们希望结出的果子能带头结出更多果子来！

一点感想：我喜欢与年轻人工作，因为有机会观察神赋予他们的才能，看见他们长大以后服务人群。不管他们是不是党书记，都让我心中充满喜乐！

翻译：林行易

11. The Joys of Deep Fried Bees Versus Smoking

Fried bees is a particular food specialty of many mountain towns in Yunnan. To be precise, actually, it is deep fried, baby bee or embryonic larva. To make it more vivid, one can see the originals squirming in their flat pancake-like beehives on the streets, during fall harvest season. These wild bees are collected by farmers from the mountains, and brought to town to sell to the hungry town folk. There's nothing like wriggling worms to stimulate one's deepest appetites. When asked what fried bees taste like, I usually respond that "It tastes just like fried crickets! And really crunchy." I might add it's not mushy, and just tickles your palate.

For the medical mission teams that came to serve in this area, it was unquestionably a "rite of passage" for new team members to crunch up these delicacies. Black or brown ones usually served piping hot, at the first welcome dinner. On one trip we had 7 delightful interactions with this insect in 10 days. For those who worry about depleting the honey-producing bees of the world, let me assure you they are not your stereotypic honey-producing bees, but a "ma-fung" (sort of wasp) type of bee, although the novice would never notice the difference. The locals take great pride in serving this delicacy whenever there is an important meal (lunch and supper, not breakfast, thankfully). And there is a big

11. 油炸蜜蜂的乐趣与抽烟

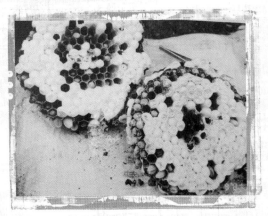

在街上贩售的扁平蜂窝
Flat beehives sold on the street

在云南山区，炸蜜蜂是一道独一无二的特色食品。明确地说，它是经过油炸的蜜蜂宝宝或胚胎幼虫。说得更生动一点，就是在秋收季节，街上到处都可以看到像薄饼般的蜂窝内有无数幼虫在蠕动着。这些野生蜜蜂是农夫们在山上采收的，然后运到镇上卖给饕客。没有什么东西比**蠕动的**幼虫更能刺激你的食欲。当有人问，炸蜜蜂是什么味道时，我通常会回答："像油炸蟋蟀一样，蛮脆的。"我还可以加上一句，**不会**黏糊糊的，很能搔动人们的味觉。

对于来到此地服事的医务队，新队员毫无疑问必须经历这番"洗礼"，就是说要吃上这个脆脆的美味佳肴。那些黑色或

point made about how nutritious it is (lots of protein, and probably "full of anti-cancer value", they say).

华盛顿州西雅图艺术家 Lily Heinzin 的作品
by Artist Lily Heinzin, Seattle, WA

Against this "exotic" cultural background, it is perhaps not surprising that there was an encounter with another deeply entrenched cultural habit: smoking. Smoking comes in the great rich, Yunnan variety (the main produce of the province), or the pricey "higher class" American models (think Marlboroughs). Often smokers use yellow fluffy powder impacted into large bamboo water pipes, said, of course, though unconvincingly, to reduce the nicotine level, etc.

When we first arrived in the town, smoke was literally blown directly into our faces in an affectionate manner. Cigarettes were offered in a packet, along with our welcome cup of tea, and a tangerine or banana. Plus the offices of the hospital's leading doctors were often smoke-filled, in spite of an obvious large "**no-smoking**" sign.

I approached this carcinogenic problem creatively. Fanning furiously did not seem to make any points (but did make one feel better). Turning on the electric fan in cool weather just seemed odd to the locals. Refusing a good cigarette bordered on being rude, especially since every male doctor around us had a cigarette dangling over the ear, just in case he needed a nicotine relief shot.

We warred on the lecture front: every team had an anti-smoking lecture. We went to the middle and high schools to teach about the "evils of smoking". We performed puppet shows. We did skits where each team

褐色的虫子在第一次的欢迎晚餐时就会吃到,端上桌时通常是热腾腾的。有一次,我们十天内就与这种昆虫有七次"美妙的互动"。对于那些担心全世界的蜜蜂会被用尽的人,我向你保证,这种蜜蜂不是你想像中那种会产蜜的蜜蜂,而是一种叫"蚂蜂"(黄蜂的一种)的蜜蜂,一般人是不会注意到它们的差异的。当地人觉得能在重要的餐会(午餐和晚餐,还好不是早餐)端上这道美食是件很自豪的事。他们会强调这道美食是多么有营养(含丰富的蛋白质,他们还说也许"有很高的抗癌价值")。

在这种异国文化背景之下,想都想得到,还有另一个流传已久的风俗,那就是抽烟。烟有两种:浓郁的云南品种(烟草是云南主要的农产品),或者是较昂贵的美国品牌的高档货(例如是万宝路牌)。抽烟的人往往把黄色的碎粉末挤压进一条大竹管子里,说是为了减低尼古丁的浓度等等,但此说法不具说服力。

当我们第一次来到这个镇上,随处可见的烟直接迎面袭来。包装的香烟会与欢迎茶一起摆上,外加一个蜜柑或香蕉。即使有一个显眼的牌子挂在那里写着**"不准抽烟"**,医院几位主要医师的办公室总还是烟雾弥漫。

我很有创意地处理这个致癌物的问题。猛搧扇子好像没什么用(但它让我觉得舒服一点)。在凉爽的天气开电风扇对当地人来讲好像有点怪异。谢绝抽烟可能会被认为没有礼貌,尤其是我们身边每位男医生的耳朵上总是挂着一根烟,在需要尼古丁舒缓时就可以派上用场。

member represented a disease related to smoking – heart attack meant falling on top of the students, hacking noisy cough meant emphysema, walking with a limp meant paralysis from stroke, coughing up blood over a student meant lung cancer. Falling down flat and dying with a cigarette dangling from the mouth was usually enthusiastically received, especially when draped dramatically with a white cloth. Sometimes we did one of these dramas in the hospital. We announced that this was to let the doctors critique the skits, "to improve the presentation before the kids." Afterwards, we asked the audience of doctors (50% of whom were smokers) to comment. One doctor declared "the leadership needs to lead on this issue." Another declared "from tonight I'll stop smoking." Did we detect a change in the air?

A small barometer of this possible change was our official escort. When we first met him, he often produced clouds of smoke at dinnertime, especially it seemed, if I was sitting next to him. Quietly he changed his habits to only smoking after dinner outside the door. Then quietly he was not smoking around us. After a while, many of our dinner conversations easily turned to the evils of smoking, and the desirability of stopping. We could now talk about the difficulty of quitting, and the value of nicotine patches; and advice on techniques for quitting. The perils of passive smoking then came up, and a great deal of banter, especially from our female members: "you should stop," "you can stop", "please stop", to "if you stop...."

So it was inevitable that the confluence of cultural norms occurred one fateful evening. A vivacious member of our team, who was able to talk to anyone and could eat most anything, to our total surprise, balked at the crème de la crème dish, fried bees. We pleaded, cajoled, laughed, bantered, and were nearly giving up, when some genius hit on the link.

我们是在讲台上发动战争的：每一组都要举办反烟害的演讲。我们到初中及高中教导学生"抽烟的害处"。我们表演木偶戏，也演短剧。在短剧里，每位队员代表一项与抽烟有关的疾病——跌倒在学生身上代表心脏病发作，很大声的干咳代表肺气肿，跛行代表中风后引起的半边身体麻痹，在学生身上吐血代表肺癌。他们一般很喜欢看到的一幕是，死人**平躺着，嘴巴还叼着一根烟**，特别是当病人身上戏剧性地盖了一块白布的时候，反应最热烈。有时候我们会到医院表演这些短剧。我们声称来医院表演是为了让医师们评论这些短剧，让我们表演给儿童看时能有所改进。表演之后我们请这些医师们（他们有一半人都抽烟）提供意见。有一位医师说："领导层需要继续关注这个议题。"另外一位说："今晚我就戒烟。"从他们的反应，我们是不是嗅到空气中有一股改变之风呢？

　　官方派来的招待员可说是测量这种改变的小小晴雨表。我们刚认识他时，发现他总是在晚餐吃饭时间吞云吐雾，特别是他坐我旁边的时候。渐渐地，他改成晚餐后在门外抽烟。后来他竟然不在我们面前抽烟了。不久，我们晚餐的谈话内容很自然就变成抽烟的毒害和戒烟的意愿。后来我们就谈到戒烟的困难、尼古丁贴片的用处，以及就戒烟的技巧提出忠告。我们也谈到二手烟的危险，很多女性成员戏谑地对当地的医生们说："你应该戒烟"，"你可以戒烟"，"请你戒烟"，到"如果你戒烟……"等。

"Heidi, if you eat these bees, Doctor Escort will stop smoking." After a stunned silence all around, we all applauded. After a long pregnant pause, in the most Christian spirit of sacrifice, tempered with a good scoop of steamed rice, our martyr swallowed the luscious bees.

One verse from the Good Book encourages us. "When you enter a town and are welcomed, eat what is set before you." (Luke 10:8) Even if strange, I assume. Fortunately there is no recommendation to inhale cigarette smoke!

竹子做的烟筒
Bamboo smoking pipes

11. 油炸蜜蜂的乐趣与抽烟
11. The Joys of Deep Fried Bees Versus Smoking

因此，在那个至关重要的晚上，不可避免的文化冲突就发生了。我们队里有一位活泼的成员，她很健谈，几乎什么东西都敢吃，所以，她竟然不肯吃这道美食中的美食**炸蜜蜂**，令我们非常惊讶。我们恳求她，用甜言蜜语哄她，笑她，作弄她都没有用。正当我们快要投降的时候，某个天才竟想到一个点子。

"海蒂，如果你把这些蜜蜂吃掉，招待医生就答应戒烟。"一时之间，全场一片寂静，紧接着鼓励的掌声响起。过了好久好久，我们的烈士以基督徒最高尚的奉献精神，和着一大汤匙的饭，把味道甘美的蜜蜂吞下肚。

短剧的一幕：抽烟导致死亡
Death from smoking skit

圣经有一节经文鼓励我们："无论进哪一城，人若接待你们，给你们摆上什么，你们就吃什么。"（路十 8）我想，就算食物很奇特我们也得吃。幸好没有人建议我们吸二手烟！

翻译：林行易

89

12. Counterfeits

Usually we are upset when a product we buy turns out to be counterfeit or "fake". We may also think of counterfeit money, counterfeit birth certificates, and counterfeit licenses. And those living in the West are often aghast at the thought of counterfeit anything.

One day I was traveling in China, a doctor came up to me and breezily announced to me "your book, the bible in the newborn nutrition world has been counterfeited." This book *Nutrition Requirements in Preterm Infants*, had been officially translated into Chinese and sold well in China. She announced the counterfeit of this translation so cheerfully, that at first I was quite surprised, but she followed quickly and said, "This is a great kind of recognition." She explained, "People only counterfeit good things, and so this means that your book is now recognized as worthy of being counterfeited."

In the next city, another doctor came up to me and just as excitedly actually showed me the counterfeit copy of the book. She asked me to autograph it. Which I did so. She emphasized, "It will now be available to many more people, so you should be happy! And yes! It shows it is a great book!"

When I reported this to my book publisher in America, his comment was, "I don't know whether I should be laughing or crying." I told him, "You should definitely laugh." I explained the "logic" and he was at loss for words. His reaction was not related to royalties, since we had already

12. 仿冒品

我们买到仿冒品时通常会觉得很生气。我们也许会想到伪币、伪造的出生证明，还有伪造的执照。住在西方国家的人，对任何的仿冒行为都会感到很惊吓。

有一天我在中国旅行，有一位医生走过来，很轻松地向我宣布："你那本被公认为新生儿营养权威的书被盗印了。"这本名为《早产儿营养》的书已经获授权被翻译为中文，在中国也有不错的销量。起初，她那种愉悦的神情令我觉得相当奇怪，但她接着又马上说："那是一种肯定。"她解释说："人们只仿冒好东西，因此这表示你的著作被公认为值得仿冒。"

在下一个城市，另一位医生向我走过来，同样兴奋地给我看一本拙劣的盗版本。她要求我在书上亲笔签名。我照做了。她还强调："现在有更多人可以看到你的书，所以你应该高兴。不错，这表示你的书是一本好书！"

我把这件事告诉我在美国的出版商，他无奈地说："我不知道我该笑还是该哭。"我告诉他："你绝对应该笑。"我把这个"逻辑"解释给他听，他却穷于辞令。他的反应和版税无关，因为我们早已经放弃了版税。他只是觉得事情很奇怪。

given away the royalties anyway. It just seemed strange.

I must confess that when I was a child, my family actually had a counterfeit version of the *Encyclopedia Britannica*, which at that time was hugely expensive overseas. Indeed I learned a lot from that encyclopedia, of course, for which I am indeed grateful. We also had the *Dorland's Medical Dictionary* in counterfeit form at home, even when I was a teenager. By the time I was in medical school, this famous dictionary was freely available in counterfeit form to all medical students on the campus.

I am not in favor of counterfeits, but the humor is there. I remember an interchange in Thailand between a Mandarin speaking shopper, and a seller whose native Chinese language was Swatow (Chaozhou). There is actually a great concern about fakes in Asia, so the buyer asked, "Is this for real? (*Zhen de ma?*)" The Chaozhou seller explained indignantly "*Jia de, Jia de*" which in the Mandarin would be: "This is false, false!" But in Chaozhou language it would be: "this is correct, correct" or "this is real, real". So a "counterfeit" also could depend on the language.

There is a remark by renowned Asian theologian-evangelist Stephen Tong: the reason that there are so many copies and versions floating around about the Jesus faith, is He is so true that everybody wants to copy Him. People copy Rolexes and Pradas, because they are high quality and high reputation, but no one would counterfeit an inferior watch or inferior handbag – what would be the point of copying these other products?

At least counterfeits could prompt good intellectual discussions.

原英文版本
The original English version

92

12. 仿冒品
12. Counterfeits

原中文翻译版本，不是仿冒品，大家兴奋地拿着的才是仿冒品
The original Chinese translation version, NOT a counterfeit, with the counterfeit one excitedly shown

坦白说，我小时候家里就有一套盗版的《大英百科全书》，当时那套书在国外是非常昂贵的。我确实从那套百科全书学到很多知识，至今令我非常感激。我十几岁时，家中就拥有盗版的《多兰氏医学字典》。到了我读医学院时，医学院的每个学生都可以很容易拿到这本著名医学字典的盗版本。

我不赞同仿冒品，但幽默就在此。我记得在泰国有一段买卖双方的对话，购买者说的是普通话，贩卖者讲的是潮州话。仿冒品在亚洲是个大问题，于是买方问："真的吗？"潮州籍的贩卖者愤然解释："*jiade, jiade*"。在普通话中，"*jia*"这个发音的意思是"假"，就是假货的意思。但在潮州话中，"*jia*"这个发音的意思却是"正"，就是真货的意思。因此，是真货还是假货，还得看对方说的是什么语言。

亚洲著名的神学家兼布道家唐崇荣博士说过：世界上有许多关于耶稣信仰的冒牌货，原因是耶稣太真实了，人人都想假冒祂。有人会仿冒劳力士手表及普拉达皮包，因为这些东西品质高，声望高，但没有人会去仿冒一个劣质的手表或包包——仿冒这些劣质品有什么价值呢？

至少仿冒品可以激发良性的思考讨论。

翻译：林行易

13. Cockroaches and Humility

低微的蟑螂可以折磨很多人
The lowly cockroach, tormentor for many

I went to school in Hong Kong. In order to get into the only medical school in Hong Kong, we had to pass a tough series of exams which included a hands-on biology "Practical Exam". In this test I had to dissect the salivary glands of a cockroach, and put it on a glass slide for evaluation. Fortunately, cockroaches in the Far East are generally larger than those in the United States. But the salivary glands are still very, very small! And they are tissue thin. Basically they are "see through" translucent, and very fragile.

So here I was, taking the hands-on exam. It was summer, and very hot and humid, a typical "sub-tropical" island weather. The ceiling fans were on full blast, since air conditioning was not generally available. With great care, I managed to finally dissect out the very dainty, fragile, tiny

13. 蟑螂与谦卑

　　我曾在香港读书。为了进入香港唯一的医学院，考生们必须通过一连串艰深的考试，包括一个要亲自动手的"实用生物学考试"。在这个考试里，我要解剖蟑螂的唾腺，把它放在镜片上，再作鉴定。幸好，远东的蟑螂通常比美国的蟑螂大。但即使如此，唾腺还是极其微小的！它薄得难以想像。基本上，蟑螂的唾腺是透明的，并且很脆弱。

　　于是，我去参加考试了。那时候是夏天，天气又湿又热，就是那种典型的亚热带岛屿气候。那时空调还没有那么普及，考场里天花板上的电风扇都开到了最大档。我小心翼翼地把那个小巧、脆弱而微小的透明体解剖了，并轻手轻脚地放在镜片上，准备好在显微镜底下检视它。

　　正当我把这片组织平放在镜片上时，一阵可怕的风从天花板上的电风扇吹过来，我发现我那宝贵的唾腺已经被吹到地上了。我疯狂地蹲下去想要把这片唾腺组织从地上刮回来。当然，那意味着整个脆弱的唾腺现在是乱七八糟的了。根本就不是本来那个美丽的组织，像一棵有很多枝子的树儿。

translucent salivary gland, and began to place it gingerly on top of a small glass slide, ready for inspection underneath the microscope.

To my great horror, at the moment in which the tissue was laid out on the glass slide, a waft of air came through from the ceiling fan, and I realized my precious salivary glands had flown to the ground. Frantically, I stooped down to try to scrape it off the ground. Of course that meant the whole fragile gland was now "a mess". It looked nothing like the expected beautiful salivary glands, with many fine branches coming off a tree.

I hurriedly summoned the Examiner- Inspector, and appealed to her "sense of justice". She gave me a stare and shrugged her shoulders and walked on. Of course I failed the Practical Exam and, therefore, since I messed up on one of the exams, I failed the entire exam. I could not get into medical school, and for one whole year I hung around in high school, clearly identified as the "Head Prefect who could not get into medical school". The Head Prefect was a very responsible position in the British school system. It was, to put it mildly, embarrassing and humiliating.

But to my great surprise, that year was an excellent year, where I grew spiritually and learned many lessons of life. It was just great to take my time, study quietly, not be in the lime-light, and learn many little lessons of humility. I learned to be more patient with those around me. Definitely, I no longer had a sense of superiority! These lessons have carried me through many difficult subsequent years.

We just never know what life throws at us. Often many things seem terrible at the time, but in retrospect they are important steps along life's path. Romans 8:28 says, "And we know that in all things God works for the good of those who love him, who have been called according to his purpose." It's very true!

13. 蟑螂与谦卑
13. Cockroaches and Humility

我仓皇地把考试官请来，祈求她给予"公正的裁决"。她盯了我一眼，耸耸肩就走了。当然，实用生物学这门考试我就考砸了，因为我有一科考坏了，整个考试就不及格了。因此我没能考上医学院。其后的一整年，我在中学无所事事，被贴上"没有考上医学院的总领袖生"的标签。"总领袖生"在英国的教育体系上是责任重大的职位。客气地说，这件事和它造成的冲击很令人尴尬，令人丢脸。

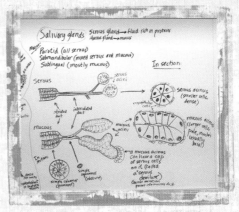

人的唾液腺已够小，可想而知蟑螂的有多小
Human salivary glands are minute enough, imagine that from a cockroach

但令我惊奇的是，那年其实是很棒的一年，我在灵性上成长了，也学会了生活上大大小小的功课。我放慢脚步，静静地读书，不在乎能不能在镁光灯下出风头，也学习了很多谦卑的小功课。我学会如何对周遭的人更有耐心。我肯定已经不觉得自己特别优越了！这些功课带着我度过无数艰难的岁月。

我们真的无法预测生命会带给我们什么。很多当时看来是很糟糕的事情，待回过头来想，往往就是我们人生路上重要的脚步。罗马书八章 28 节说："我们晓得万事都互相效力，叫爱神的人得益处，就是按他旨意被召的人。"那是多么真实啊！

翻译：林行易

14. A Baby is Born

I'm a neonatologist, a doctor who specializes in newborn infants. When I see a newborn baby, my instinctive reflex is always "this is a miracle", even though I've seen thousands of newborn babies. This response is common for many delivery room workers. Everyone is so excited to see a new baby, to hear the first cry, and exclaim "is it a boy or a girl?!"

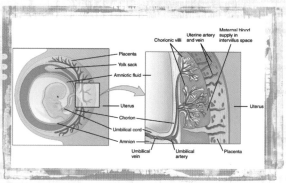

精美复杂的胎盘
The beautifully complex placenta

And then suddenly the lifeline (umbilical cord) is cut. For months and months, the umbilical lifeline, connected to the placenta and mother, has supplied all the **nutrients** that the baby needed from her mother, and transferred all the baby's **rubbish back into the mother**. It is a remarkable system that has kept the baby alive for many months and in

14. 新生儿

我是一位新生儿科医生，专门研究新生儿医学。虽然我见过成千上万的新生儿，但每当我看到又一个新出生的小生命时，我的第一反应仍会是："真是一个奇迹！"当然，这也是产房工作人员的常见反应。每当大家听到小婴儿的第一声啼哭时，所有人都会异常兴奋地问："是男孩还是女孩？"

当小婴儿顺利出生后，脐带就会被切断。脐带这条生命线数月来一直连接着胎盘和母体，负责从母亲那里输送宝宝需要的所有**营养物质**，又将宝宝的**排泄物运回母体**那里。很难想像，就是这个奇妙的系统在孕育生命的几个月里，一直维持着宝宝的生命与健康。所以，我经常和孩子们开玩笑说："每当你想到自己的出生，你就要紧紧抱着妈妈，对她说：'我爱你！在我还没出生**前**，妈妈你不仅提供我一切所需，甚至不曾抱怨，还照单全收我的排泄物。'"

令人惊讶的是，就在这脐带被剪断的瞬间，成千上万的激素、酶和化学物质马上开始运作，婴儿的全部生理过程产生了**革命性**的变化，比如心脏、肺、血管、肾脏、大肠、小肠、大脑等器官，在数分钟内变得完全不一样。这些器官的变化是毫

such great shape. I often joke to children that, when you think of your own birth, you need to hug your mother tightly and say: "Mom, I love you; even **before** I was born, not only did you give me all that I needed, you even took all my dirty diaper stuff without complaining."

But now, at the moment of birth, the cord is cut, and amazingly, thousands upon thousands of hormones, enzymes and chemicals spring into action, and change remarkably; within minutes, there's a **total revolution** in physiology. The heart, the lungs, the blood vessels, the kidneys, the intestines, the brain, nothing is the same anymore. But all of it is beautifully synchronized and perfect; it's much better than a Swiss watch; everything is dynamically perfect.

I deal with sick small babies; the smallest baby that we took care of and survived was II oz! Yet remarkably, as we manage these sick small babies, the major task is often not to really cure anything. Basically we aim to **not ruin** the amazing physiology that happens at this time. As doctors looking after premature infants, our main job is to **prevent** things from happening that could harm the baby. For example, we try to give them adequate nutrition (my field of research), and support for the lungs, so that at the right time, all the systems are permitted to turn on; whether it be hormones, enzymes, chemicals, they all ultimately **should** "turn on"! Even though they were not originally "planned" to turn on this early, **if** we do **not harm** the baby, "**the systems**" turn on to meet the new reality of early birth.

So where does this **precision** reside? What is the program of this fantastic computer that can drive all of this? The huge modern day understanding of the complexity of molecular biology quickly reminds us to wonder, who is the **master genius** who designed it all? Who put in all the biologic "master switches"? What prompts an earlier switch when

无瑕疵、有条不紊地进行着，这种完美即便是标榜精准度的瑞士钟表也是望尘莫及。

我专责于医治生病的小宝宝。你知道吗，我曾经医治并救活的婴儿最小的只有 310 克（六两多）！值得一提的是，对于这些生病的小婴儿，医生的主要任务往往不是医治，而是通过医疗手段，辅助并确保**不破坏**或干扰这个神奇生理系统的形成。例如，我们会尽量提供充足的营养（这是我的研究领域）及支援肺部功能，以确保所有系统都能在最佳的状态与时机下启动。无论是激素、酶，还是其他化学物质，最终都**要**投入运作行列！只要确定**不伤害**早产儿，**这些系统**都会自动提早投入运作行列，以满足早产儿的生理需要。

那么，这个**精准度**从何而来？能主导这一切的又是个怎样精确的程式呢？以现代科学来理解这繁复庞杂的分子生物学时，我们就不禁思考：是什么样的**天才**设计了这一切？是谁组装了整个生理主控系统？是什么为早产儿提早启动这些生理系统？是谁想出这个神奇的系统，创造了生命的奇迹，展开一个又一个深具意义和喜乐的新生命？

翻译：孙珺、彭瑞锦

babies are born prematurely? Who thought of this amazing system that results in the miracle of birth, to begin a life with potential for meaning and joy!?

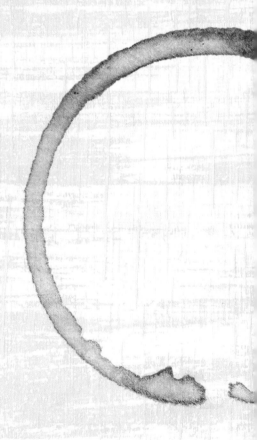

14. 新生儿
14. A Baby is Born

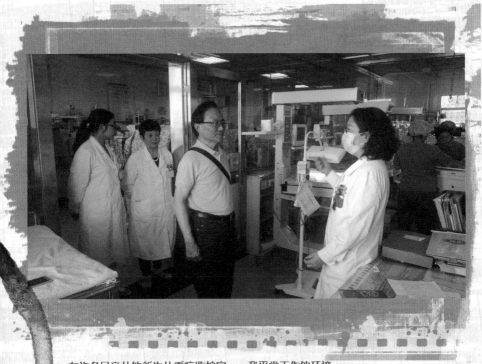

有许多早产儿的新生儿重症监护室——我平常工作的环境

In my normal environment, the Neonatal Intensive Care Unit,
with many premature infants

15. A Near Death Experience

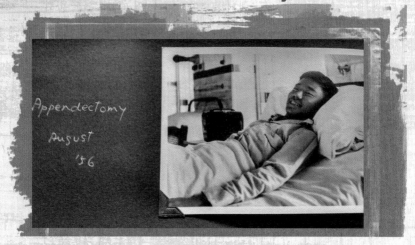

二十世纪五、六十年代我父亲给我做阑尾切除手术时典型的香港医院病房
Typical Hong Kong ward of the 1950s and 60s, when my father removed my appendix

One day, a few days after I started my internship at the Queen Mary Hospital in Hong Kong, I was doing morning rounds on my ward. In those days, it was common to have 20 beds or so per ward, and overflow patients had to sleep on cots. Some cots were even in open air balconies adjoining the ward rooms.

Suddenly one of my patients, who had a **brain tumor**, got up from his cot and walked briskly towards the balcony. I thought that was strange and instantly tensed up. Indeed, he went straight to the railing and started to climb over the railing.

I dashed immediately toward him, shouting, "What are you doing? What are you doing?"

15. 与死亡面对面

有一天早上，我正在医院的病房里巡查，那时我刚开始在香港玛丽医院实习不久。在那个年代，每个病房里放 20 张床是司空见惯的事，多出的病人还要睡在可折迭的帆布床上，有些帆布床甚至要放在病房旁边的阳台上。

突然，我有一名患**脑肿瘤**的病人从帆布床上起来，径直走向阳台。我觉得奇怪，也开始紧张起来，果不其然他直接走到阳台的栏杆前并试图翻过去。

我马上冲过去，大声喊到："你要干什么？你要干什么？"不出我所预料，他真的准备要跳下去，我立刻紧紧抓住他的两只胳膊。我意识到，他比我要重的多，这样下去后果不堪设想。我开始恳求他："不要跳，不要跳。"然而，他没有理会我，只听到他最后说了一句"我走了"，就翻过栏杆。

当他悬在半空的时侯，我一把紧紧地拽着他的前臂，这时他的生命全在于我能否紧紧抓住他。不一会，我看到他病号服上的袖套开始滑落，我也明显感觉到他从我手中缓缓向下滑。这时，五层楼以下的地面开始聚集了人群，他们惊恐地望着我们，我也**惊恐地**看着这病人的**面**，仿佛感觉楼下的人群变得模

Sure enough, he acted like he was ready to jump, so I gripped both his forearms. He was a heavier person than I was, and I sensed that this was not going to end well. I pleaded with him, "Don't jump, Don't jump!" ("*Mm ho tieu, Mm ho tieu!*") However, he ignored me and quickly stepped out into the air, with his final words to me, "I'm leaving." ("*Ngor tsau la*")

So there I was, hanging on to both his forearms while he was dangling in the air, his only connection with life being my grip. Soon I could see the hospital gown sleeves on his forearms beginning to slip and my hold clearly slipping. By this time, a crowd was gathering at the ground level, 5 stories below. They were all watching us in horror, while I was watching the **face** of this man **in horror**, with the blur of the crowd as background. I prayed a silent prayer, not really knowing what else to do, except hanging on.

Suddenly a nursing "sister" (in the British system, head nurses are called "sisters") with a better size than mine, ran over. She grabbed one of the man's forearms, and I shifted my whole effort to the other forearm. She yelled, "Pull, pull, pull!" and for some Herculean reason, we dragged him up while he was hanging in mid-air.

Fortunately, he did not really fight back. A few more people by now had overcome their shock and rushed to the scene. We were able then to jerk his whole body up and over the railings, and onto the balcony, where he was suitably subdued and taken to . . . I don't really remember where.

All I could think of was, "What happened?" I sat down dazed, a brand new intern at his first major test. Staring at death in the face.

Author's note to you: while life and death are often out of our control, our eternal destiny depends on our choice. A great place to start is to consider Giver of life.

糊。我做了一个默祷，除了坚持下去外，我不知道还能做什么。

突然，一个比我力气大的护士长跑了过来。她抓住了病人的一只前臂，于是我用尽全力去拉他的另一只前臂。她大声喊到"用力拉，用力拉，用力拉"，不知道从哪里来那么大的力气，我们竟然把他从半空中拉了上来。

二十世纪三十年代，我父亲就读我后来上的同一所医学院，他危险地坐在那个时代典型的阳台边缘——小心！

In the 1930s, my father had earlier attended the same medical school as I later did, perched precariously on typical balcony of the times: be careful!

幸好他没有再去挣扎，那些惊魂否定的人缓过神来，也都跑到了现场。我们用尽全力把他的整个身体拉过栏杆，拉到方便应对的阳台上，然后把他带到……我都不记得带到哪里了。

我能想到的就只是："刚才发生了什么事"。我茫然地坐在那里，一个毫无经验的实习生遇到的第一次大测试，竟是面对死亡的震撼教育。

一点感想：虽然我们无法控制生死，但我们永恒的命运却取决于我们的选择。最好的选择就是开始去思考那位赐给我们生命的主。

翻译：张鹏远

16. Eternity in Our Genes

Some people are surprised and say, "How can anyone believe in heaven or eternity?" But actually, eternity is already **in our genes**. Generation after generation, we see the effect of eternity in our genes. Our ancestors had our genes, our descendants will have our genes, and genes never seem to die!?

A fetus begins as a speck that is invisible, and then it grows and grows into a full fetus in the mother's womb, and then a baby, then a child, then a "terrible toddler", to a child, to all of us. Then we in turn have babies, who in turn continue generation after generation to repeat this. Our genes continue on and on.

When basic scientists study cells in "culture lines", in the laboratory, they call these cells "immortal cells". Which means basically, that, well... they are **immortal**.

When a person goes to the Sequoia National Park in California, and looks at the trees, an amazing realization occurs: the General Sherman tree is 6,000 tons, 272 feet tall, 32 feet in diameter, and has 4,000-year history! Well...4,000 years ago, the genes were there, but the genetic material remains today, just another glaring example of the "eternity" principle.

God has already given us a **taste** of eternity in our very being, and in nature. So it should not be difficult to understand eternity! King Solomon,

16. 基因显永恒

DNA 链
DNA strand

有些人会觉得不可思议："你怎么会相信天堂和永生呢？"
然而事实是，永生或永恒就**在我们的基因里**。在一代一代人的
繁衍中，我们可以在基因里看见永恒。我们的祖先有我们的基
因，我们的后代会有我们的基因，基因好像不会消亡！？

　　胎儿开始时是一个看不见的点，后来在母亲的子宫内长成
胎儿，然后成了婴孩，再后是难缠的学步阶段，之后变成孩子，
最后长大成人。我们继而也生孩子，一代代周而复始。我们的
基因不断延续下去。

one of the wisest man on earth, said in Ecclesiastes 3:11, "God has set eternity in our hearts." And Pascal, the great mathematician has said, "There's a void in man's heart that only God can fill." That void can be filled with God's eternity.

Think about that.

佘曼将军树
General Sherman tree

16. 基因显永恒
16. Eternity in Our Genes

　　基础研究科学家在实验室做细胞培养基实验时，常称这些培养基细胞是不死的细胞，意味着这些细胞基本上是……**不死的。**

　　当你走进加州的红杉国家公园，看到那里的大树，你会有这样一个奇妙的感悟：佘曼将军树重 6,000 吨，高 272 英尺，直径 32 英尺，已有 4,000 年历史！天哪……4,000 年前已经有的基因，今天属同一基因的物体还在那里，又一个彰显永恒原理的例子。

　　神已经在我们自己身上，也在自然界中让我们**尝到**永恒的滋味。所以理解永恒应该不难！所罗门王是一个世上少有的聪明人，他曾在传道书三章 11 节说："神……又将**永生安置在世人心里。**"伟大的数学家帕斯卡曾说："在我们心里有一个洞，只有神才能填满。"那个洞只能被神的永恒填满。

　　请好好想想这个问题。

17. Asian Stereotype

When I arrived in the morning at the hotel in Buenos Aires, Argentina, I did a very "Asian" thing. I took my fine camera and went out to take pictures in the middle of the day. The weather was drizzly, so I decided to cross the street by going into the subway under the road. Evidently, I had been spotted taking tourist pictures, though by this time, I had stuffed my camera back into my shoulder bag.

Suddenly a woman with 3 small children in tow, on her right and left, approached me: "*Mostaza!*" She pointed to my back, sure enough there was a streak of yellow mustard down the center of the back of my jacket. Very helpfully, she took out a wad of tissue paper to try to wipe off the poor tourist's misfortune.

Having grown up in the big city of Hong Kong, my street smarts threw my antennae into high alert. I backed into a wall and tried to stop her. Trying to be even more helpful, the woman handed me her handbag to hold on to while she was busy cleaning my back. Presumably, this was done to confuse me a bit more. I held even more firmly to the shoulder strap of my bag, and used my free little finger to twirl around her handbag strap.

All this happened in a few quick seconds: 2 young men jumped out of the shadows, one on each side, and each was in my trouser pocket. My wallet in the left pocket flew out and dropped on the ground.

112

17. 对亚洲人的偏见

当我早上到达位于阿根廷布宜诺赛勒斯市的一个旅馆时，我做了一件很典型的亚洲人喜欢做的事情：中午的时候，带着我的相机到外面拍照。天空下着毛毛雨，所以我决定穿过地铁通道到街的对面。显然有人留意到我这个遊客正在拍照，虽然那个时候我已经把相机塞回了单肩包里。

突然一个妇女出现在我面前，有三个小孩跟在她左右。她指着我的后背说："*Mostaza*"，原来在我夹克后面中间的位置有一条黄色的芥末酱。她很热心地掏出一团纸巾，试图擦掉这位可怜遊客的不幸。

在香港这样的一个大城市里长大的我，在街头学来的小聪明瞬间让我提高警惕。我退到一堵墙边上并试图阻止她。而为了更方便帮我，她在擦掉我身上的芥末酱的同时，还把她的手提包给我让我拿着。这举动大概是让我更加摸不着头脑，我把单肩包的带子拉的更紧了，同时用我的小拇指勾住她的手提包。

接下来发生的事情只花了短短几秒钟：有两个年轻人不知道从哪里跳出来，一边一个，两个人都把手伸进了我口袋里，瞬间放在我左边口袋里的钱包飞了出来，掉在地上。

In a move which surprised myself, I suddenly made a "kung fu" crouch, backed against the wall, hands angled in front of me, and shouted the classic "Hai!" as loudly as I ever could.

Presumably, all my attackers had watched many Chinese kung fu movies, since their response was dramatic. They all left instantly, and my wallet was left on the ground where it had landed. This was the first and last time I ever exercised my kung fu heritage.

A thought: We are all affected by what we have read and seen in our lives. Each experience causes us to mold our thinking. We also develop stereotypes about others, especially those from a different cultural background. These stereotypes often cause us to react in stereotypical ways to others, which often may be totally inappropriate. Fortunately, God sees into our souls and knows exactly who and what we are!

"For the Lord seeth not as man seeth; for man looketh on the outward appearance, but the Lord looketh on the heart" (1 Samuel 16:7b).

外国人在火车站时应时刻保持警惕
Foreigners should always be careful at train stations

114

　　我的下一个举动让我自己也吃了一惊。我突然背靠着墙蹲了一个马步，两只手交叉挡在前面，并且用尽全身力气很经典地大喊了一声"嘻！"

　　可能攻击我的这几个人看过太多中国功夫电影，他们的反应充满了戏剧性——马上跑掉，我掉在地上的钱包还是在原地没动！这是我第一次也是最后一次使出我的"武术遗产"。

　　一点感想：我们都会被生活中所看到、所读到的影响，每个经历也会塑造我们的思维。我们对其他人常会产生一种成见，尤其是当他们来自不同的文化背景时，更容易产生这种成见。这些成见常常导致我们用有色眼镜去看待他人，这往往是不可取的。幸好造物主能看透我们的灵魂，知道我们的本质和心思意念！

　　"耶和华不像人看人：人是看外貌；耶和华是看内心。"（撒母耳记上十六 7）

翻译：张鹏远

他以许多种方式露面
He shows up in many ways

115

18. Asian Hospitality

野猪晚餐第一步：烧毛
Boar dinner initial step: singeing the hair

Asians love to express their hospitality in many interesting ways. Barnabas, a missionary to tribal groups in the mountains of Northern Thailand, had many heavy meals of special pork. It is a habit of many tribes to slaughter a pig for visiting dignitaries. Normally, they do not have much meat, but during such visits the pig becomes a great sign of their warmth and hospitality.

The pig, which is really a wild boar, is finished off by a spear to the heart, sometimes right in the middle of the church yard, allowing the blood to drain into the muddy channels of the church grounds. Then the villagers take a torch made of twigs and branches to singe off the hair. Finally, they take a scraper of metal or wood and scrape off the hair (sort

18. 亚洲人的热情好客

亚洲人喜欢通过许多别开生面的方式来表达自己的热情好客。

在泰国北部山区给部落群体传道的巴拿巴牧师饱餐过很多特别的猪肉宴。杀猪迎贵客是许多部落的习惯。平时他们不常吃肉，但在欢迎宾客时，猪肉就成为他们热情好客的一大标志。

所指的猪其实就是野猪，有时就在教堂院子的中央用矛把它穿心刺死，让血液排入教堂地面泥泞的沟渠里。之后村民用树枝制作的火炬来烧毛。最后他们用一个金属或木质的刮具把毛刮掉（差不多都掉了吧）。肉随后被切成块，带着闪闪发光的脂肪和猪皮，甚至还有猪毛。如此美味的猪肉是特意提供给高贵的客人享用，而到访的牧师就经常获得这种慷慨的接待。

在我们完成短宣旅程离开泰国之后数天，我给巴拿巴打电话问他怎么了。他说他感觉有些胸痛，正开车去医院。果不其然，他心脏病发作。村民终于注意到对牧师的**慷慨**款待还会导致他心脏病发作。看过许多教育碟盘后，村民开始意识到慷慨的行动也要有节制。

of). Then the meat is cut up in chunks of glistening fat, plus the skin and even some authentic hair. This delicious pork is served especially to the distinguished visiting guest, and the visiting pastor is often the recipient of this generosity.

One day, just a few days after we had left Thailand after a short term mission trip there, I called up Barnabas on the phone and asked him how he was. He said that he was feeling some chest pain and was driving now to the hospital. Sure enough, he had a heart attack. It was finally brought to the attention of the villagers that being so **generous** to your pastor might lead to heart attacks. After many educational DVDs, the villagers have begun to recognize that generosity has limits.

For years when we went to the Yunnan town of Luquan and Xundian, we were given feasts of fried bees. One time we were given fried bees on 7 occasions in 10 days. The villagers were showing their greatest hospitality by offering this rather expensive dish. We learned to dive right into it and found out that it's really a fantastic food. The key is not to eat bees with mature wings, but to gobble the bees down when they are in the larva stage! When asked what does it taste like, I often reply that "it tastes just like fried crickets". Which, if you have never eaten it, simply means that you have been "culturally deprived".

At the end of my internship, we were married immediately, and my new bride and I promptly proceeded on our quasi-honeymoon trip to America. We stopped by in different cities, along the way. In Tokyo, we were the special guests of a friend who invited us to her home for a spectacular dinner. All the family members were sitting around the table, on the ground. In the middle of the room was the best dish of all, raw fish – sashimi. Except that I had only recently finished medical school and, in my eyes and in my brain, were floating all kinds of ugly tapeworms,

18. 亚洲人的热情好客
18. Asian Hospitality

曾有几年每次去云南的禄劝和寻甸时，人家都会给我们吃油炸蜜蜂。其中有一次，在十天内我们吃了七次油炸蜜蜂。村民提供这道相当昂贵的菜肴，以表达他们最盛情的款待。我们试着吃

晚餐前刮野猪皮
Scraping boar skin pre-dinner

起来，感觉这真是一道美食。关键是不要吃已有成熟的翅膀的蜜蜂，只吃那些还是蛹的蜜蜂！若有人问我味道怎样，我通常会回答："它的味道就像油炸蟋蟀。"要是你从来没有吃过油炸蟋蟀，那你见的世面就太少了。

我结束实习后就马上结婚，和我的新娘开始我们到美国的半蜜月之旅。一路上，我们在不同的城市逗留。在东京，把我们看为上宾的一个朋友邀请我们到她家里吃了个丰盛的晚餐。全家人围着桌子席地而坐。放在房间中央的是最好的菜式：生鱼片。只可惜我最近才医学院毕业，在我的眼前和脑里浮现的是各种丑陋的绦虫，包括鱼绦虫。我吞了吞口水、停下来、愣着，最后一个令人震惊的评论脱口而出，像是："对不起，我不能吃生肉。"在场的人难以置信，亦无言以对。我面红耳赤，羞愧难当，不知道怎样才能钻入地缝里。在这样的情况下，我设法板着面孔。女主人平静下来，打发人出去，最后买来一个美式汉堡包。这是我在饮食文化上最沉重的打击，我从来都没有忘记它。从那时起，我知道我基本上不得不尽量去吃摆在我

including fish tapeworms. I gulped and stopped and stared, and finally, I blurted out a really shocking comment to them like: "I'm so sorry, I can't eat raw meat." There was stunned disbelief and silence of all who were there. I did not know how to disappear into the ground. Totally red, embarrassed and really ashamed of the situation, I managed to keep a straight face. The hostess composed herself, and sent someone out who finally came back with an American McDonalds hamburger. It was the lowest culinary blow of my life, and I have never forgotten it. From that point onward, I knew that I basically had to try to eat whatever was laid before me, which is what the good book says actually.... Secretly however I have dropped some special foods to pets and eager wandering dogs. They deserve good food too.

With an open attitude, things such as fried rats, boiled white earthworms, wriggling fresh live shrimp, and yes, fried crickets can be enjoyed, although really cooking it well, and especially frying it crisply, is definitely a great enhancement of taste.

面前的食物，这其实也是圣经的教导……不过背地里，我也丢一些难吃的给宠物和垂涎遊走的狗儿。它们也该享受点美食。

　　如果有一个开放的态度，哪怕是油炸老鼠、煮白蚯蚓、扭动着的新鲜生虾，对了，还有炸蟋蟀都可被享用。配上好的烹饪，尤其是把它用油炸脆，肯定能大大地提升味道。

翻译：权克明

油炸是最好的（开胃菜：蜂蛹）
Fried is best (Bee larva pre-dinner)

121

19. Where is Cincinnati ?

Over the years, many people I first met in the American academic world assumed I was from California, since Asian Americans seemed to predominate from that part of the country. So they are surprised when I say "I'm from Cincinnati."

After my arrival in the US, I worked as a pediatric resident in Chicago at the Michael Reese Hospital from 1966 to 1969. In my 3rd and final year I was also a part time fellow, focusing specifically on work in the nurseries. I was fascinated with neonatology and neonatal research, and this arrangement allowed me to do my research at night, while I was covering the nurseries.

My mentor and supervisor sat me down one day and said, "I'm going to UCLA to head up Neonatology there. You go down to Cincinnati for 2 years, get fully trained and then join me as faculty member."

That sounded really good to me. "Yes, sir," I said, and paused. "But where is Cincinnati?" Actually my understanding of US geography was very good, having grown up from childhood reading all about America, the land where my ABC (American-born Chinese) mother came from. But Cincinnati, where was that?

I found out that Cincinnati is a wonderful place. I have lived more than 40 years in Cincinnati now and traveled all over the US and many cities in the world, but Cincinnati is "home". The people in Cincinnati are courteous and friendly, and we have a wonderful Chinese (language)

19. 辛辛那提在哪？

多年来，我在美国学术界第一次遇到的人，有许多都认为我是来自加利福尼亚，因为亚裔美国人似乎主要是来自该国的那个地区。所以当我说"我来自辛辛那提"，他们就很惊讶。

来美后我于 1966 年至 1969 年在芝加哥的迈克尔里斯医院作儿科住院医生。第三年也是最后一年，我是个兼职的研究员，专门研究婴幼儿护理。我迷上了新生儿学和新生儿的研究，而这样的安排让我能在夜里从事婴幼儿护理的同时，又做我的研究。

一天，我的导师和主管叫我坐下来，说："我要去加州大

Church which even includes an All Nations (English language) Congregation. I often play tour guide to many international visitors who come to Cincinnati to study.

First, I bring them to Spring Grove Cemetery! You see in Asia, often graves are very unpleasant places. But in Cincinnati, we have a lovely cemetery, the second largest private cemetery in the country. The landscape is artistically designed, and the many lakes, fountains and statues make it look more like a beautiful park than a cemetery. It's an opportunity to explain that the worldview here includes a place called heaven, so death need not be a sad thing, but a transition to a new life!

Another two favorites I love are the views from the oldest church in town, Immaculata, which overlooks the charming Ohio River from a stunning viewpoint; and the church of the Holy Basilica, which is a replica of Notre

冬季的春天树丛墓园
Spring Grove in the Winter

Dame. One doesn't have to travel to Paris, since we have a beautiful replica right in town! And the stories in the superb stained glass of both churches provides a great testament to history.

There are some great museums of significant meaning in town: the unique Underground Railroad Freedom museum, which shows well the

学洛杉矶分校作新生儿科系主任。你去辛辛那提好好锻炼两年，然后到我这儿来作教员。"

　　这听起来真好。"好的，老师"，我说，然后停了一下，又问："可是辛辛那提在哪？"其实我的美国地理知识非常好。我的母亲是在美国出生的华人，我从小就阅读所有关于美国的东西。但是，辛辛那提！？它到底在哪儿！？

　　我后来发现辛辛那提是一个美妙的地方，在辛辛那提我一住就是 40 多年。我也曾跑遍了美国和世界上许多城市，但辛辛那提是我真正的"家"。辛辛那提人礼貌且友好。我们有一个美好的华语教会，在这个教会里还有万国（英语）会众。我又经常给很多前来辛辛那提学习的国外学者作导游。

　　首先，我带他们去春天树丛墓园！在亚洲，坟墓通常是一个令人非常不安的地方。但在辛辛那提，我们有一个可爱的墓园，它是美国第二大的私人墓地。墓地的景观设计充满艺术色彩，加上众多的湖泊、喷泉和雕塑，使它看起来更像是一个美丽的公园而非一个墓地。参观墓园让我有机会讲解在我们的世界观里，有一个叫做天堂的地方，因此死亡不一定是一件悲哀的事，而是展开新生命的一个过渡！

　　另外两个我最爱的景观是从两座教堂所看到的风景：在市内最古老的教堂圣母无原罪教堂，你能由一个惊人的制高点俯瞰动人的俄亥俄河；而神圣大教堂就是巴黎圣母院的一个复本。所以，你不必专程去巴黎，我们城内就有一个美丽的复本！两

slavery struggle and emancipation story, in the city where many slaves crossed the Ohio River to escape to freedom; the Creation museum, the only one in the US depicting a literal biblical history of Creation; the Air Force museum in Dayton an hour away commemorating the Wright brothers of Dayton, Ohio. And many other great museums. Find out about Cincinnati by visiting us!

So if you are still wondering, "Where is Cincinnati", hop on to a plane and come visit us!

春季的春天树丛墓园
Spring Grove in the Spring

个教堂内精湛的彩绘玻璃窗饰所描绘的故事为历史作了美好的见证。

市内有几个很有意义的博物馆：独一无二的地下铁路自由博物馆展出黑奴斗争和解放的历史，许多黑奴就是在这个城市越过俄亥俄河投奔自由的。创造博物馆在美国也是独一无二的，它是按照圣经历史来描绘创造的过程。代顿的空军博物馆是位于约一个小时车程的地方，它是纪念俄亥俄州代顿市的赖特兄弟。其他许多博物馆举不胜举。要了解辛辛那提的话，请来探望我们！

所以，如果你还在纳闷，"辛辛那提在哪儿？"赶快搭飞机来游览吧！

翻译：权克明

Postscript

I have lived in conservative Midwest Cincinnati for 47 years, but have traveled more than 3 million frequent flyer miles around the world. But in 2016 we moved to Seattle where my American roots really began (but that's another story). I am "technically" retired. For example, more than 20 years ago, I took my first **"early retirement"** from taking care of premature babies, to start a medical mission in Southwestern China. More than 10 years ago, I took my **"second retirement"** to work with young people on my vision of Youth for All Nations, in Cincinnati. Please pray now for my **"third retirement"**, which should focus on savoring more coffee and stories with you. You could also get a foretaste of these stories by visiting Reggietales.org, where my new stories will be "test run", while I transition into my likely final phase of life. Come back again for the next book....

后记

我在辛辛那提保守的中西部地区生活了 47 年，但却在世界各地旅行，超过 300 万飞行里数。2016 年，我们搬到西雅图——我在美国的根真正开展之处（但这是另一个故事⋯⋯）。名义上，我已经退休了。例如 20 多年前，我第一次"**提早退休**"，放下照顾早产儿的工作，在中国西南部开展医疗服务。十多年前，我"**第二次退休**"，在辛辛那提与青少年一起为"万国青年"的异象工作。现在，请为我"**第三次退休**"祷告：要专注与你一起品尝更多的咖啡和故事。当我渐渐进入可能是人生的最后一个阶段时，你也可以在 Reggietales.org 这个网站先睹为快，我的新故事会在网站上供人"试读"。请再回来读我的下一本书⋯⋯

翻译：Eileen

About the Author

The author Reginald Tsang, is a medical doctor who specializes in premature infant care (Neonatology). He was Director of the Division of Neonatology at the Cincinnati Children's Hospital Medical Center for 15 years. He has published more than 400 scientific articles and papers related especially to infant and perinatal calcium and nutrition research. In 1994 he took early retirement to answer the call for medical missions, co-founding the Medical Services International organization to work in rural minority areas in Southwest China. In 2004 he took his second retirement to serve his home church, the Cincinnati Chinese Church where he is founding elder, serving especially in youth and missions ministry. Professor Tsang is affectionately called "Uncle Reggie" by 3 year old kids to 70 year old adults, since he loves to chat and tell many stories related to his many travels overseas. He has logged in 3 million miles of flight travel, taught 10,000 pupil hours of English especially to Chinese village kids, and helped bring more than 5,000 short term people units on mission trips to China and Southeast Asia.

作者简介

　　作者曾振锚是一名专门从事早产儿护理的医生。他曾在辛辛那提儿童医院医学中心担任新生儿科主任 15 年。他发表了 400 多篇科学文章和研究论文，特别是关于婴儿和围产期钙和营养的研究。1994 年，为回应医疗服务使命的呼召，他提早退休，与伙伴共同成立了国际医疗服务机构（Medical Services International, MSI），服事中国西南地区少数民族的农村。2004 年，他第二次退休，回到他的母会辛城教会（他也是创办该教会的长老之一）致力参与青少年和宣道的事工。从三岁小孩到 70 岁的长者都亲切地称曾教授为"Uncle Reggie "，因为他喜欢聊天，又会讲很多他海外旅行的故事。他的飞行里数已超过 300 万英里，教授过一万教学时数的英语，特别是教导中国乡村的小孩子，又有分带领 5,000 多人次到中国和东南亚参与短期海外宣道工作。

Some storytellers tell us stories almost anyone else could spin. Uncle Reggie is a storyteller with tales so unique that just to sit and listen to him is a rare experience. So just get started reading *Coffee with Uncle Reggie* and soon you will find yourself travelling via the vehicle of imagination both around the world and even back in time, as it were, learning about amazing people and history-shaping events!

Bon voyage!

> Don Richardson, veteran missiologist,
> author of *Peace Child* and many other classic missions books

With wit, wisdom and winsomeness, Uncle Reggie shares stories that will touch and perhaps transform your heart. A great read!

> David Stevens, MD, M.A. (Ethics),
> Chief Executive Officer, Christian Medical & Dental Associations USA

If a picture is worth a thousand words, then a story is worth a million pictures! Uncle Reggie has been telling wonderful stories over coffee for years! Now he invites you to encounter God's great work from these touching and enlightening stories in the comfort of your own home. :)

> Jenny Liao, Carnegie Mellon student, and planner of the first Reggietales.org

有些人讲的故事几乎任何人都可以编出来。曾叔叔所讲的故事是如此独特，能坐下来听他讲故事已经是一个难得的经历。所以只要一开始阅读《与曾叔叔闲聊》，很快你会发现自己坐上了想像力的快车，环游世界，甚至时光倒流，认识了不起的人和塑造历史的事件！

一路顺风！

唐·理查森，经验丰富的宣教学家
《和平之子》和许多经典宣教学著作的作者

风趣、有智慧又活泼，曾叔叔分享的故事不但会触动你的心，也许更会改变它。一本很好的书！

大卫·史蒂文斯医生，文学硕士（伦理）
美国基督徒医师及牙医协会首席执行官

如果一张图片胜过千言万语，那么一个故事就能胜过100万张图片！曾叔叔多年来一直在喝咖啡时讲美妙的故事！现在，他邀请你安坐家中，从这些有启发性的感人故事中，认识造物者伟大的工作。：）

Jenny Liao，卡内基梅伦大学学生
第一个 Reggietales.org 网站的策划者

Coffee with
Uncle Reggie
与曾叔叔闲聊
我们的新生儿科教授

The author invites you to read more Uncle Reggie stories at his bilingual website: Reggietales.org.

Publishing and printing of this book is supported by YFAN Heritage Foundation. You can support this effort through USA tax deductible donations to: YFAN heritage foundation, c/o 1002 Eastgate Dr., Cincinnati, OH 45231 Check made out to: YFAN heritage foundation, Memo line: YFAN literature mission fund

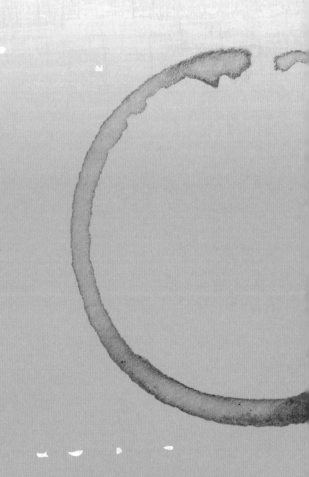

作者诚邀读者登上他的双语网站，阅读更多曾叔叔的故事：Reggietales.org。

本书的出版和印刷获得 YFAN Heritage Foundation 赞助，读者可以捐款支持，捐款收据可申请减免美国税项。支票请邮寄至：
YFAN heritage foundation, c/o 1002 Eastgate Dr., Cincinnati, OH 45231, USA
支票抬头：YFAN heritage foundation；备注（如适用）：YFAN literature mission fund